BISCUITS AND COOKIES

BISCUITS
AND
COOKIES

LORNA RHODES

PHOTOGRAPHS BY SUE JORGENSEN

BEDFORD EDITIONS

Published by Bedford Editions Ltd.

129-137 York Way

London N7 9LG

United Kingdom

ISBN 0 86101 732 3

CREDITS

Managing Editor: ANNE MCDOWALL

Editor: VERONICA SPERLING

Designer: PETER BRIDGEWATER

Photographer: SUE JORGENSEN

Home Economist: LORNA RHODES

Stylist: MARIA KELLY

Typesetting: VANESSA GOOD

Illustrator: LORRAINE HARRISON

Index: ALISON LEACH

Colour reproduction: P & W GRAPHICS PTE. LTD.

PRINTED IN ITALY

CONTENTS

◆ ◆ ◆

Introduction   6

Classic Cookies   8

Luxury Treats   34

Tray Bakes   54

Festive Cookies   72

No-bake Cookies   86

Index   94

INTRODUCTION

❖ ❖ ❖

Everyone loves freshly baked cookies – the delectable aroma of baking is so irresistible. As well as being pleasurable to eat, cookies are easy and fun to make and, with so many different ingredients to combine together, the variety of cookies is almost endless.

This book is a collection of some of the many cookies that can be created at home for a fraction of the cost of bought ones; it is surprising just how many can be made from a small amount of mixture. Make them for family and friends, or give as a present; wrapped in pretty paper, they make popular gifts, especially at holiday times.

Cookies are also ideal to make for fund-raising events such as fêtes and bazaars. The ingredients need not be expensive, but the rewards are great and home-made cookies always sell out fast, which proves their appeal.

HINTS ON INGREDIENTS

The recipes in this book use everyday ingredients that can be bought in most supermarkets. Always choose good-quality fresh ingredients when buying butter, nuts and chocolate. Measure ingredients carefully, because the amounts given in the recipes are balanced to give good results. Be guided by the yield stated in the recipe; if you make many less or more, they may turn out too large or too small.

BUTTER: Many recipes call for unsalted butter, which has a fresh and creamy taste and gives an excellent flavour and result. Some recipes that would normally have salt added use salted butter instead, and a few others use margarine. Butter always gives a better flavour but margarine can be used for dairy-free cookies. For best results have butter and eggs at room temperature (unless otherwise stated).

SUGARS: The recipes always indicate the type of sugar to use. Many use unrefined brown sugars, which have more flavour and give tastier results than refined brown sugar. Muscovado sugar needs to be sifted, as often small lumps form during storage. Golden caster and granulated sugar have a subtle buttery flavour, which will make cookies particularly delicious. If unrefined sugar is not available, then white sugar or soft light and dark brown sugar can be used.

CHOCOLATE: When choosing chocolate for these recipes, always use a good-quality one with a high cocoa solids content. Avoid cake-covering types of chocolate; these have a high sugar and vegetable fat content and will not give good results. Handle carefully when melting; warm slowly so as not to overheat.

PREPARATION HINTS

When making creamed mixtures you can use a wooden spoon, electric mixer or food processor. It is important not to over beat, because if the mixture is overworked it will become too soft and the cookies will spread too much during baking. Add dry ingredients carefully, using pulse on food processors to avoid overworking the dough.

Check your oven manufacturer's handbook for any instructions on shelf positions. Generally, for gas ovens, the top half will give best results, electric ovens need to be pre-heated before baking and fan-assisted ovens will bake four trays of cookies at a time. Check temperatures, as fan-assisted ovens need to be turned down slightly and generally cook more quickly. Baking times in recipes are given as a guide; every oven differs slightly in temperature, so check cookies before the stated cooking time is up.

CLASSIC COOKIES

The easiest cookies to make in this chapter are 'drop' cookies, for which the soft dough is spooned directly onto the baking sheet. Drop cookies tend to spread during baking and the shape will often be irregular. The texture is also variable; it can be soft and chewy or crisp, like the popular Chocolate Chip Cookie.

Shaped cookies, such as Ginger Snaps and Honey Jumbles are also very straightforward to make – the dough is moulded with cool hands, but care must be taken not to overhandle the mixture as the dough will toughen during baking.

For rolled mixtures, such as Vanilla Sugar Cookies, the dough must be stiff and often requires chilling so that you can roll it evenly before using a cutter. Too much flour used in rolling out will result in tough cookies. When no liquid is added, for example in shortbread, the mixture will require plenty of kneading before it is rolled out. The thinner you roll the dough, the crisper the baked cookies will be.

Piped cookies look very special and require a little more time and skill. Metal nozzles give a more defined shape than plastic. Alternatively the dough can be pressed out with a mechanical biscuit press.

Refrigerator dough is a useful standby to have so that cookies can be baked at your convenience. A wide variety of flavourings can be used in the dough, which is chilled until it is firm enough to be cut into thin slices.

CONTENTS

◆ ◆ ◆

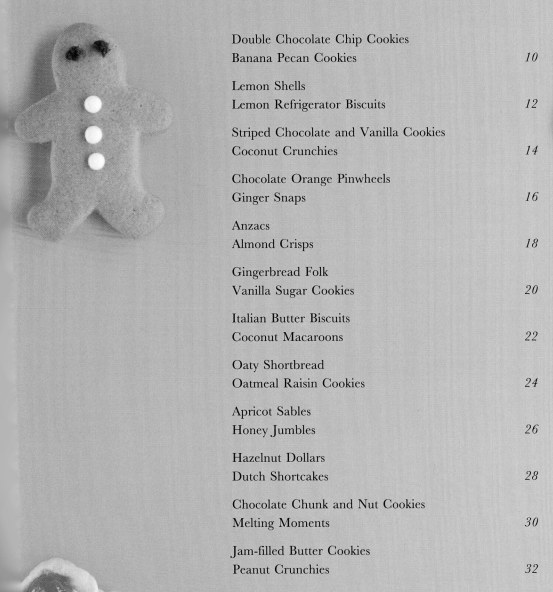

Double Chocolate Chip Cookies
Banana Pecan Cookies   *10*

Lemon Shells
Lemon Refrigerator Biscuits   *12*

Striped Chocolate and Vanilla Cookies
Coconut Crunchies   *14*

Chocolate Orange Pinwheels
Ginger Snaps   *16*

Anzacs
Almond Crisps   *18*

Gingerbread Folk
Vanilla Sugar Cookies   *20*

Italian Butter Biscuits
Coconut Macaroons   *22*

Oaty Shortbread
Oatmeal Raisin Cookies   *24*

Apricot Sables
Honey Jumbles   *26*

Hazelnut Dollars
Dutch Shortcakes   *28*

Chocolate Chunk and Nut Cookies
Melting Moments   *30*

Jam-filled Butter Cookies
Peanut Crunchies   *32*

DOUBLE CHOCOLATE CHIP COOKIES

These classic cookies, with their soft chewy texture, are absolutely delicious eaten warm. They crisp up when cooled and have a rich chocolaty flavour.

◆ ◆ ◆

75 G/3 OZ BUTTER OR MARGARINE

75 G/3 OZ GOLDEN CASTER SUGAR

75 G/3 OZ LIGHT MUSCOVADO SUGAR, SIFTED

1 LARGE EGG, BEATEN

5 ML/1 TSP VANILLA ESSENCE

150 G/5 OZ SELF-RAISING FLOUR

25 G/1 OZ COCOA

25 G/1 OZ WALNUTS, FINELY CHOPPED

175 G/6 OZ PLAIN CHOCOLATE DROPS

MAKES ABOUT 16

◆ ◆ ◆

Put the butter or margarine into a bowl with the sugars. Beat together until fluffy, add the egg and vanilla essence, and beat well again.

Sift together the flour and cocoa and fold into the mixture with the walnuts and three-quarters of the chocolate drops.

Drop heaped teaspoonfuls of the mixture onto greased baking sheets. Flatten slightly then sprinkle over the rest of the chocolate drops.

Bake at 180°C/350°F/Gas Mark 4 for 15 minutes. Cool for 2 minutes then transfer to a wire rack to cool completely.

BANANA PECAN COOKIES

Children will love the nutty banana taste of these cookies. The banana makes them slightly moist and chewy.

◆ ◆ ◆

100 G/4 OZ BUTTER OR MARGARINE

175 G/6 OZ GOLDEN GRANULATED SUGAR

1 LARGE EGG

30 ML/2 TBSP DARK RUM OR ORANGE JUICE

1 MEDIUM RIPE BANANA, MASHED

225 G/8 OZ PLAIN FLOUR

2.5 ML/$\frac{1}{2}$ TSP BAKING POWDER

100 G/4 OZ PECAN NUTS, CHOPPED

PECAN NUT HALVES TO DECORATE

MAKES ABOUT 26

◆ ◆ ◆

Beat together the butter or margarine with the sugar until creamy. Add the egg and rum or orange juice and beat again. Mix in the banana.

Sift the flour and baking powder together, mix in the nuts then add to the creamed mixture.

Drop heaped rounded teaspoonfuls onto greased baking sheets and press a pecan half onto each. Bake at 170°C/325°F/Gas Mark 3 for 18-20 minutes until lightly browned. Cool for 2-3 minutes then transfer to a wire rack to cool completely.

TOP: *Banana Pecan Cookies*
BOTTOM: *Double Chocolate Chip Cookies*

LEMON SHELLS

These light biscuits have a lovely tangy lemon flavour and make a perfect partner to either tea or coffee.

◆ ◆ ◆

100 G/4 OZ SOFT MARGARINE

50 G/2 OZ ICING SUGAR

1.25 ML/$\frac{1}{4}$ TSP VANILLA ESSENCE

30 ML/2 TBSP LEMON JUICE

15 ML/1 TBSP FINELY GRATED LEMON RIND

1 EGG YOLK

150 G/5 OZ PLAIN FLOUR

25 G/1 OZ CORNFLOUR

1.25 ML/$\frac{1}{4}$ TSP BAKING POWDER

12 GLACE CHERRIES, HALVED

GLAZE

30 ML/2 TBSP LEMON JUICE

30 ML/2 TBSP CASTER SUGAR

MAKES ABOUT 20

◆ ◆ ◆

Cream the margarine with the icing sugar until smooth. Add the vanilla essence, lemon juice and rind and egg yolk and beat again.

Sift together the flour, cornflour and baking powder, add to the creamed mixture and work together to form a soft dough.

Put into a piping bag fitted with a 1.5 cm/$\frac{1}{2}$ inch star nozzle. Pipe about 20 shells onto greased baking sheets then place a half cherry on each. Bake at 180°C/350°F/Gas Mark 4 for 12-15 minutes.

Meanwhile, mix the lemon juice and caster sugar together, brush over the biscuits while still hot, then transfer to a wire rack to cool.

LEMON REFRIGERATOR BISCUITS

The mixture for these biscuits is chilled then cut into thin slices before baking. It can also be stored uncooked in the refrigerator for a few days and used as required.

◆ ◆ ◆

175 G/6 OZ BUTTER

100 G/4 OZ CASTER SUGAR

GRATED RIND OF 1 LEMON

1 EGG, BEATEN

250 G/9 OZ PLAIN FLOUR

CASTER SUGAR AND GRATED NUTMEG TO DUST

MAKES 30

◆ ◆ ◆

Cream together the butter and sugar until very pale. Add the lemon rind and egg and beat until smooth. Stir in the flour and work together to a make a dough.

Turn onto a lightly floured work surface and knead until smooth. Form into 1 or 2 logs about 6 cm/$2\frac{1}{2}$ inches in diameter. Wrap in greaseproof paper and refrigerate at least 1 hour or until firm.

Unwrap the dough and cut off thin biscuits, placing them on greased baking trays. Bake at 190°C/375°F/Gas Mark 5 for about 12 minutes until pale golden.

Dredge with caster sugar and nutmeg while still warm. Leave to cool completely on a wire rack.

TOP: *Lemon Shells*

BOTTOM: *Lemon Refrigerator Biscuits*

STRIPED CHOCOLATE AND VANILLA COOKIES

These butter cookies are made with chocolate and vanilla-flavoured doughs which are layered and cut into strips.

◆ ◆ ◆

225 G/8 OZ BUTTER

100 G/4 OZ CASTER SUGAR

300 G/10 OZ PLAIN FLOUR

30 ML/2 TBSP COCOA

5 ML/1 TSP VANILLA ESSENCE

MAKES ABOUT 28

◆ ◆ ◆

Put the butter and sugar into a bowl and beat together until light and creamy. Add the flour and mix to make a dough. Transfer two-thirds of the dough to another bowl and work in the cocoa until evenly blended. Add the vanilla essence to the remaining piece of dough.

Roll out half of the chocolate dough to a rectangular strip 7.5 cm/3 inches wide, 23 cm/9 inches long and 1.25 cm/$\frac{1}{2}$ inch thick. Place on a large sheet of grease-proof paper.

Roll out the vanilla dough to the same measurements, lightly brush the strips with water and place the vanilla on top of the chocolate.

Roll out the remaining chocolate dough and place on top of the vanilla. Wrap in the greaseproof paper and chill for at least 30 minutes.

Grease 2 baking sheets, unwrap the dough and with a sharp knife cut thin slices about 5 mm/$\frac{1}{4}$ inch thick and place on the baking sheets. Bake at 180°C/350°F/Gas Mark 4 for 12-15 minutes. Cool for 2 minutes then transfer to a wire rack.

COCONUT CRUNCHIES

Quick and easy to make, these cookies look good topped with shredded coconut. If this is not available, use desiccated coconut instead.

◆ ◆ ◆

100 G/4 OZ SELF-RAISING FLOUR

PINCH OF SALT

5 ML/1 TSP GROUND CINNAMON

100 G/4 OZ BUTTER OR MARGARINE

100 G/4 OZ LIGHT MUSCOVADO SUGAR, SIFTED

1 EGG, BEATEN

75 G/3 OZ DESICCATED COCONUT

SHREDDED COCONUT TO DECORATE

MAKES 28-30

◆ ◆ ◆

Sift together the flour, salt and cinnamon. Cream the butter or margarine until light and fluffy, add the egg. Stir in flour and coconut until well blended.

Drop teaspoonfuls of the mixture onto greased baking sheets, allowing space for spreading, and flatten slightly with a fork. Top each one with a little shredded coconut. Bake at 180°C/350°F/Gas Mark 4 for 15-20 minutes until golden. Cool for a few moments then transfer to a wire rack to cool completely.

TOP: *Coconut Crunchies*

BOTTOM: *Striped Chocolate and Vanilla Cookies*

CHOCOLATE ORANGE PINWEELS

These cookies look very impressive with their two tone spirals. The prepared dough can be kept in the refrigerator for a few days and then cooked when needed.

❖ ❖ ❖

225 G/8 OZ BUTTER OR MARGARINE

100 G/4 OZ CASTER SUGAR

325 G/11 OZ PLAIN FLOUR

15 ML/1 TBSP COCOA

10 ML/2 TSP GRATED ORANGE RIND

MAKES ABOUT 36

❖ ❖ ❖

Cream the butter or margarine with the sugar until light and fluffy. Put half the mixture into another bowl and add 150 g/5 oz of the flour and all the cocoa. Add the rest of the flour and the orange rind to the other half of the mixture.

Form both mixtures into smooth pliable doughs. Roll each one out to a rectangle, the same size, about 20 x 28 cm/8 x 11 inch and 3 mm/$\frac{1}{8}$th inch thick.

Place the chocolate-flavoured dough on a large piece of greaseproof paper, carefully place the orange dough on top. Roll up along the length like a Swiss roll, using the greaseproof paper to guide the rolling. Wrap the roll in the paper.

Refrigerate the roll for at least 1 hour or until firm. Remove the paper and cut the dough in thin slices. Place the cookies on greased baking sheets and bake at 180°C/350°F/Gas Mark 4 for 10-15 minutes, or until golden. Cool for 2 minutes then transfer to a wire rack to cool completely.

GINGER SNAPS

These biscuits are sometimes called Ginger Nuts, probably because they are hard, but still delicious to eat.

❖ ❖ ❖

250 G/9 OZ PLAIN FLOUR

5 ML/1 TSP BICARBONATE OF SODA

15 ML/1 TBSP GROUND GINGER

2.5 ML/$\frac{1}{2}$ TSP ALLSPICE

75 G/3 OZ BUTTER

100 G/4 OZ DARK MUSCOVADO SUGAR, SIFTED

75 G/3 OZ GOLDEN SYRUP

1 EGG, BEATEN

MAKES ABOUT 36

❖ ❖ ❖

Sift together the flour, bicarbonate of soda, ginger and allspice. Set aside.

Beat the butter with the sugar and golden syrup until creamy, add the egg and beat again.

Stir in the dry ingredients and mix to form a firm and pliable dough. Take pieces of the dough about the size of a small walnut and roll each in the palm of the hand to make a ball.

Place the balls on greased baking sheets and flatten slightly. Bake at 170°C/325°F/Gas Mark 3 for 15-20 minutes, until firm. The tops should have small cracks on the surface. Cool for a few moments, then transfer to a wire rack to cool completely.

TOP: *Chocolate Orange Pinwheels*
BOTTOM: *Ginger Snaps*

ANZACS

Originally from Australia, these cookies are now famous all over the world and a favourite of many families.

◆ ◆ ◆

75 G/3 OZ ROLLED OATS
150 G/5 OZ WHOLEMEAL FLOUR
75 G/3 OZ DESICCATED COCONUT
100 G/4 OZ GOLDEN CASTER SUGAR
30 ML/2 TBSP GOLDEN SYRUP
150 G/5 OZ SUNFLOWER MARGARINE
45 ML/3 TBSP WATER
7.5 ML/1^1/$_2$ TSP BICARBONATE OF SODA

MAKES ABOUT 30

◆ ◆ ◆

Put the oats, flour, coconut and sugar into a bowl and mix together.

Put the golden syrup, margarine and water into a pan and heat until boiling. Immediately add the bicarbonate of soda, allow it to foam up then add to the dry ingredients and mix together.

Place spoonfuls of the mixture onto greased baking sheets and bake at 170°C/325°F/Gas Mark 3 for 12-15 minutes until a rich golden colour.

Cool slightly then transfer to a wire rack to cool completely.

ALMOND CRISPS

A light and crisp biscuit which will keep well in an airtight container for a few days.

◆ ◆ ◆

100 G/4 OZ UNSALTED BUTTER
75 G/3 OZ CASTER SUGAR
1 LARGE EGG YOLK
FEW DROPS OF ALMOND ESSENCE
75 G/3 OZ BLANCHED ALMONDS, LIGHTLY TOASTED
150 G/5 OZ SELF-RAISING FLOUR
CASTER SUGAR TO DECORATE

MAKES 24

◆ ◆ ◆

Cream together the butter and sugar until light and fluffy, add the egg yolk and almond essence and mix well.

Chop the almonds (not too finely) and add to the mixture with the flour. Mix together to make a dough.

Form into 24 balls and place on greased baking sheets. Take a heavy-bottomed glass, dip in caster sugar and press down each ball to flatten, dipping the glass in sugar each time.

Bake the biscuits at 180°C/350°F/Gas Mark 4 for 12-15 minutes. Cool for 1 minute then transfer to a rack to cool completely.

TOP: *Anzacs*
BOTTOM: *Almond Crisps*

GINGERBREAD FOLK

Children of all ages will love to help make and decorate these favourite cookies.

❖ ❖ ❖

450 G/1 LB PLAIN FLOUR
15 ML/1 TBSP GROUND GINGER
5 ML/1 TSP MIXED SPICE
10 ML/2 TSP BICARBONATE OF SODA
100 G/4 OZ BUTTER OR MARGARINE
100 G/4 OZ GOLDEN SYRUP
100 G/4 OZ MOLASSES SUGAR
1 EGG, BEATEN
CURRANTS
GLACE CHERRIES (OPTIONAL)
75 G/3 OZ ICING SUGAR

MAKES ABOUT 40

❖ ❖ ❖

Sift the flour into a bowl with the spices and bicarbonate of soda. Put the butter or margarine into a saucepan with the syrup and molasses sugar, heat gently until melted. Pour onto the dry ingredients, add the egg and mix together to make a dough. The dough will look sticky to begin with but will become more elastic and firm as it cools.

Roll out to about 3 mm/$\frac{1}{8}$th inch thick and cut out with gingerbread people shapes. Transfer to greased baking sheets and add currants for eyes and pieces of glacé cherries for mouth if wished.

Bake at 170°C/325°F/Gas Mark 3 for 15-18 minutes. Remove from trays and transfer to wire racks to cool.

Mix the icing sugar with 15-20 ml/3-4 tsp water to make a thick consistency. Pipe buttons, bows etc on the cooled cookies.

VANILLA SUGAR COOKIES

Cut these cookies into any shape you wish. For a children's party, try some novelty or animal shapes.

❖ ❖ ❖

100 G/4 OZ BUTTER OR MARGARINE
150 G/5 OZ PLAIN FLOUR
25 G/1 OZ CORNFLOUR
5 ML/1 TSP VANILLA ESSENCE
50 G/2 OZ VANILLA SUGAR
100 G/4 OZ ICING SUGAR
SUGAR STRANDS OR COLOURED SUGAR
CRYSTALS

**MAKES ABOUT 18-28
DEPENDING ON SIZE OF CUTTERS**

❖ ❖ ❖

Rub the butter or margarine into the flours until the mixture resembles fine breadcrumbs. Add the sugar and essence and work together to make a firm dough. Lightly knead until smooth, wrap and chill for 1 hour until firm.

Roll out the dough, not too thinly, and cut into chosen shapes. If using sugar crystals, brush the cookies with egg white and sprinkle over the sugar. Place on greased baking sheets and bake at 180°C/350°F/Gas Mark 4 for 10-12 minutes. Allow to cool for 1 minute then lift onto a wire rack to cool completely.

Mix the icing sugar with a little water to make a thick icing, place a small teaspoonful on each cookie and spread evenly. Decorate with sugar strands if wished.

TOP: *Gingerbread Folk*
BOTTOM: *Vanilla Sugar Cookies*

ITALIAN BUTTER BISCUITS

This recipe uses a biscuit press, a marvel-lous invention for making different shaped biscuits, just by changing the cutting disc. Once mastered, two different coloured doughs can be placed in the tube to give some inter-esting effects. The dough can also be rolled out and cut with small biscuit cutters.

◆ ◆ ◆

175 G/6 OZ UNSALTED BUTTER

75 G/3 OZ CASTER SUGAR

FEW DROPS OF ALMOND ESSENCE

1 EGG YOLK

250 G/9 OZ PLAIN FLOUR

CASTER OR ICING SUGAR TO DUST

MAKES ABOUT 50

◆ ◆ ◆

Cream together the butter and sugar until light and fluffy. Add the almond essence then gradually add the flour to make a firm dough.

Take about a quarter of the dough and knead lightly, form into a log shape and place inside the cylinder of the biscuit press. Attach the desired shape cutter and press out onto greased baking sheets.

Bake at 190°C/375°F/Gas Mark 5 for 10-12 minutes or until lightly browned. Transfer to wire racks to cool and sprinkle with caster sugar while warm, or with icing sugar when cold.

COCONUT MACAROONS

An unusual recipe for macaroons, the addition of marzipan gives these cookies a scrumptious flavour.

◆ ◆ ◆

100 G/4 OZ MARZIPAN

75 G/3 OZ CASTER SUGAR

100 G/4 OZ DESICCATED COCONUT

3 EGG WHITES

5 GLACE CHERRIES, QUARTERED

MAKES ABOUT 20

◆ ◆ ◆

Put the marzipan into a food processor with the sugar and work together until the mixture resembles fine crumbs.

Whisk the egg whites until stiff, carefully fold in the marzipan crumbs and the coconut. Drop spoonfuls in heaped mounds onto baking sheets lined with either rice paper or non-stick baking parchment.

Place a quarter of cherry on each and bake at 150°C/300°F/Gas Mark 2 for about 25 minutes until golden.

If using rice paper break it off around each cookie, if using parchment paper, the macaroons will peel off eas-ily. Cool on a wire rack. Store in an airtight container for up to a week. Do not freeze.

TOP: *Italian Butter Biscuits*
BOTTOM: *Coconut Macaroons*

OATY SHORTBREAD

There are many recipes for shortbread. This one, which is quite crunchy, is a delicious biscuit to have with afternoon tea.

◆ ◆ ◆

175 G/6 OZ UNSALTED BUTTER

75 G/3 OZ GOLDEN CASTER SUGAR

100 G/4 OZ PLAIN FLOUR

PINCH OF SALT

5 ML/1 TSP GROUND CINNAMON

75 G/3 OZ ROLLED OATS

SUGAR TO DUST

MAKES 12 PIECES

◆ ◆ ◆

Beat the butter and sugar together until light and creamy. In another bowl mix the dry ingredients together then add to the creamy mixture. The texture will be crumbly and loose. Turn into an ungreased 23 cm/9 inch loose-bottomed flan tin. Dip fingers in a little extra rolled oats and press the mixture evenly into the tin.

Smooth the top and prick all over with a fork. Bake the shortbread at 180°C/350°F/Gas Mark 4 for about 40 minutes. While still warm, take a sharp knife and score the shortbread into 12 wedges. Sprinkle the top with sugar and leave to cool in the tin. When cold the shortbread can be cut into portions.

OATMEAL RAISIN COOKIES

These wholesome cookies, which use high-fibre ingredients, would make a healthy addition to packed lunches and picnics.

◆ ◆ ◆

100 G/4 OZ SUNFLOWER MARGARINE

75 G/3 OZ MEDIUM OATMEAL

175 G/6 OZ WHOLEMEAL PLAIN FLOUR

5 ML/1 TSP GROUND CINNAMON

75 G/3 OZ GOLDEN GRANULATED SUGAR

100 G/4 OZ RAISINS

1 LARGE EGG, BEATEN

A LITTLE MILK

MAKES 20

◆ ◆ ◆

Put the margarine into a bowl with the oatmeal and flour and rub together to form a crumbly mixture.

Stir in the cinnamon, sugar and raisins then mix together with the egg and a little milk to make a firm dough.

Form into 20 balls and place on greased baking sheets. Press down with a fork and bake at 180°C/350°F/Gas Mark 4 for 15-20 minutes until firm to the touch.

Allow to cool slightly then transfer to a wire rack to cool completely.

TOP: *Oaty Shortbread*
BOTTOM: *Oatmeal Raisin Cookies*

APRICOT SABLES

These sables (meaning sand) are the French
version of an English shortbread.
The biscuits should be light and crumbly.

◆ ◆ ◆

225 G/8 OZ PLAIN FLOUR

100 G/ 4 OZ ICING SUGAR

175 G/6 OZ UNSALTED BUTTER

50 G/2 OZ GROUND ALMONDS

50 G/2 OZ READY-TO-EAT DRIED APRICOTS,

FINELY CHOPPED

1 LARGE EGG YOLK

15 ML/1 TBSP APRICOT JAM

MAKES ABOUT 30

◆ ◆ ◆

Sift the flour and icing sugar into a bowl. Rub in the butter until the mixture resembles fine crumbs. Stir in the ground almonds and apricots then bind together with the egg yolk.

Lightly knead the dough on a barely floured surface until smooth, then wrap in cling-film and chill in the refrigerator for 1 hour.

Roll out the dough to a thickness of 5 mm/$\frac{1}{4}$ inch and cut out biscuits with a glass or biscuit cutter 5 cm/2 inches in diameter. Place on greased baking sheets and refrigerate for 30 minutes.

Put the apricot jam into a small greaseproof piping bag and pipe a small blob on each biscuit. Bake at 170°C/325°F/Gas Mark 3 for 15-20 minutes until pale golden. Cool slightly then transfer to a rack to cool completely.

HONEY JUMBLES

These biscuits are sometimes known as
Bosworth Jumbles. The story goes that the
recipe was dropped by King Richard's cook
on the battlefield of Bosworth.

◆ ◆ ◆

150 G/5 OZ BUTTER

50 G/2 OZ GOLDEN CASTER SUGAR

75 G/3 OZ CLEAR HONEY

1 EGG, BEATEN

300 G/10 OZ PLAIN FLOUR

50 G/2 OZ GROUND ALMONDS

30 ML/2 TBSP CLEAR HONEY, WARMED

GOLDEN CASTER SUGAR TO DUST

MAKES ABOUT 24

◆ ◆ ◆

Cream the butter, sugar and honey together until light and pale. Gradually work in the egg, flour and ground almonds.

Work the mixture into a dough. Take pieces of dough weighing 25 g/1 oz each and roll each into a smooth ball, then into a sausage shape 10 cm/4 inches long. Form into 'S' shapes and carefully place on greased baking sheets.

Bake at 180°C/350°F/Gas Mark 4 for 10-12 minutes until golden. Brush with the warmed honey and sprinkle with sugar. Lift off and cool on a wire rack.

TOP: *Honey Jumbles*
BOTTOM: *Apricot Sables*

HAZELNUT DOLLARS

Toasting the hazelnuts really helps to bring out the flavour in these biscuits. Some supermarkets sell hazelnuts ready chopped.

◆ ◆ ◆

150 G/5 OZ UNSALTED BUTTER

75 G/3 OZ CASTER SUGAR

5 ML/1 TSP VANILLA ESSENCE

175 G/6 OZ PLAIN FLOUR

2.5 ML/$\frac{1}{2}$ TSP BAKING POWDER

50 G/2 OZ HAZELNUTS, LIGHTLY TOASTED AND FINELY CHOPPED

50 G/2 OZ PLAIN CHOCOLATE

M A K E S   A B O U T   2 4

◆ ◆ ◆

Beat the butter and sugar together until light and creamy. Add the vanilla essence. Sift the flour with the baking powder and mix into the creamed mixture with the nuts.

Work together to make a dough and knead lightly on a floured surface until smooth. Wrap in cling-film and chill for 1 hour.

Roll out thinly and cut into rounds with a 7.5 cm/3 inch fluted cutter. Carefully place the cookies on greased baking sheets and bake at 190°C/375°F/Gas Mark 5 for 6-8 minutes.

Cool slightly then transfer to a wire rack to cool completely. Melt the chocolate and allow to cool. Place in a small greaseproof bag and drizzle over the biscuits. Leave to set.

DUTCH SHORTCAKES

A classic cookie mixture which can be piped in different shapes. Rich in flavour and crumbly in texture, these shortcakes make a lovely gift presented in an attractive tin or box.

◆ ◆ ◆

225 G/8 OZ UNSALTED BUTTER, SOFTENED

75 G/3 OZ CASTER SUGAR

2.5 ML/$\frac{1}{2}$ TSP VANILLA ESSENCE

225 G/8 OZ PLAIN FLOUR

50 G/2 OZ CORNFLOUR

CASTER OR ICING SUGAR TO DUST

M A K E S   A B O U T   2 4 - 2 7

◆ ◆ ◆

Beat the butter and sugar together until very light and creamy. Add the vanilla essence.

Sift the flour and cornflour together then add to the creamed mixture and mix to make a soft dough.

Put the dough into a piping bag fitted with a large star nozzle and pipe out whirls or 'S' shapes onto greased baking sheets.

Bake at 180°C/350°F/Gas Mark 4 for 15-20 minutes until very lightly golden. Transfer to a rack to cool. Either sprinkle with caster sugar while warm or dust with icing sugar when cool.

TOP: *Dutch Shortcakes*
BOTTOM: *Hazelnut Dollars*

CHOCOLATE CHUNK AND NUT COOKIES

The combination of chocolate and nuts in these melt-in-the-mouth cookies is quite irresistible.

❖ ❖ ❖

100 G/4 OZ BUTTER

100 G/4 OZ GRANULATED SUGAR

75 G/3 OZ LIGHT MUSCOVADO SUGAR, SIFTED

2 EGGS, BEATEN

10 ML/2 TSP VANILLA ESSENCE

250 G/9 OZ PLAIN FLOUR, SIFTED

5 ML/1 TSP BAKING POWDER

100 G/4 OZ PLAIN CHOCOLATE,
CUT INTO SMALL CHUNKS

100 G/4 OZ HAZELNUTS, ROUGHLY CHOPPED

M A K E S   1 6

❖ ❖ ❖

In a bowl cream together the butter and sugars until light in consistency. Beat in the eggs and vanilla essence. Sift in the flour and baking powder and stir in the chocolate and nuts.

Place dessertspoonfuls on greased baking sheets and flatten slightly. Bake at 180°C/350°F/Gas Mark 4 for 10-12 minutes.

Cool for 2 minutes then transfer to a wire rack to cool completely.

MELTING MOMENTS

Children love to make these cookies, probably because they are easy to prepare, but more because they are so good to eat.

❖ ❖ ❖

100 G/4 OZ BUTTER

75 G/3 OZ CASTER SUGAR

1 EGG YOLK

5 ML/1 TSP VANILLA ESSENCE

150 G/5 OZ SELF-RAISING FLOUR

25 G/1 OZ CORNFLAKES

10 GLACE CHERRIES

M A K E S   2 0

❖ ❖ ❖

Cream together the butter and sugar, beat in the egg yolk and vanilla essence. Gradually work in the flour to make a soft dough. Chill for 30 minutes.

Divide the mixture into 20 balls. Crush the cornflakes slighty and place on a plate. Take each ball and gently press one side onto the cornflakes, flattening them a little. Place on greased baking trays, cornflake side up, and place a half a cherry in the centre of each biscuit.

Bake at 190°C/375°F/Gas Mark 5 for 15-20 minutes until golden brown. Cool for 2-3 minutes, then transfer to a wire rack to cool completely.

TOP: *Chocolate Chunk and Nut Cookies*
BOTTOM: *Melting Moments*

JAM-FILLED BUTTER COOKIES

*Cut these cookies in any shape,
depending on the cutters available – even
plain round cookies will look good.*

◆ ◆ ◆

225 G/8 OZ PLAIN FLOUR

75 G/3 OZ ICING SUGAR

2.5 ML/$1/_2$ TSP BAKING POWDER

100 G/4 OZ BUTTER

1 EGG YOLK

2.5 ML/$1/_2$ TSP VANILLA ESSENCE

STRAWBERRY OR RASPBERRY JAM

ICING SUGAR TO DUST

M A K E S   A B O U T   1 6

◆ ◆ ◆

Put the flour, icing sugar and baking powder into a
bowl, add the butter and rub in to resemble fine
crumbs. Mix to a dough with the egg yolk and essence.
Knead until smooth then wrap in cling-film and refrigerate for 1 hour until firm.

Roll out thinly and use a 5-7.5 cm/2-3 inch diameter
cutter to cut out the cookies. Place on greased baking
sheets. Cut the centres out of half of the cookies with a
small round or shaped cutter.

Bake at 190°C/375°F/Gas Mark 5 for 8-10 minutes
or until light golden in colour. Cool for a few moments
then transfer to a wire rack to cool competely.

When cold, spread jam on the whole cookies, top with
the other cookies and dust with icing sugar.

PEANUT CRUNCHIES

*Peanuts are an all-time favourite with
many families. Quick and easy to make,
these cookies can always have a place in
the cookie tin.*

◆ ◆ ◆

100 G/4 OZ BUTTER

100 G/4 OZ CRUNCHY PEANUT BUTTER

100 G/4 OZ LIGHT MUSCOVADO SUGAR, SIFTED

100 G/4 OZ ICING SUGAR

1 LARGE EGG, BEATEN

2.5 ML/$1/_2$ TSP VANILLA ESSENCE

225 G/8 OZ PLAIN FLOUR

5 ML/1 TSP BAKING POWDER

75 G/3 OZ PEANUT KERNELS, ROUGHLY CHOPPED

M A K E S   A B O U T   3 0

◆ ◆ ◆

Put the butter into a bowl with the peanut butter and
both sugars, beat together well. Add the egg and vanilla
essence and beat again.

Sift together the flour and baking powder, add to the
creamed mixture and mix until well blended. Take
heaped teaspoonfuls of the mixture and roll into balls.
Press each onto the chopped nuts, flattening down
slightly at the same time.

Place the cookies on greased baking sheets then bake
at 180°C/350°F/Gas Mark 4 for 10-12 minutes. Cool
for 2 minutes, then transfer the cookies to a wire rack
to cool completely.

TOP: *Peanut Crunchies*
BOTTOM: *Jam-filled Butter Cookies*

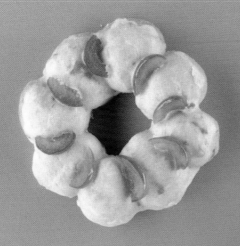

LUXURY TREATS

With the addition of other ingredients, such as glacé cherries, marzipan, dried fruit and nuts, simple basic recipes can be turned into very special cookies, and using unusual shaped cutters and sandwiching layers of biscuit together adds an extra touch of luxury. The cookies in this chapter are ideal for special occasions and many of them make delicious accompaniments to fruit fools, sorbets and ice-creams. They also make delightful gifts, wrapped in pretty paper or presented as a selection arranged in a basket.

Most cookie recipes only require basic kitchen equipment; use scales and measuring spoons and cups for accurate weighing. The most important item is the baking sheet or tray. For even baking and browning, a strong aluminium sheet gives excellent results. It is worth having more than one baking sheet, as it is much easier to spoon and shape the mixture all at once and cook at the same time. Use melted butter for greasing, but do not overgrease or the cookies will become too dark underneath. Non-stick baking parchment is essential to prevent rich doughs and meringues from sticking to baking sheets. It is also useful when rolling out a mixture that is difficult to handle – just place the dough between two sheets of the paper.

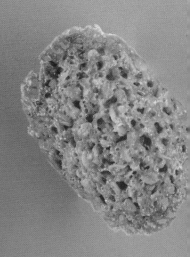

CONTENTS

◆ ◆ ◆

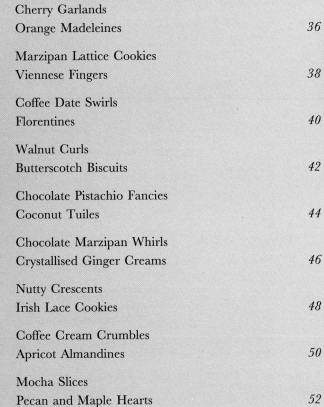

Cherry Garlands
Orange Madeleines   36

Marzipan Lattice Cookies
Viennese Fingers   38

Coffee Date Swirls
Florentines   40

Walnut Curls
Butterscotch Biscuits   42

Chocolate Pistachio Fancies
Coconut Tuiles   44

Chocolate Marzipan Whirls
Crystallised Ginger Creams   46

Nutty Crescents
Irish Lace Cookies   48

Coffee Cream Crumbles
Apricot Almandines   50

Mocha Slices
Pecan and Maple Hearts   52

CHERRY GARLANDS

An attractive cookie, which has a slightly fragrant rosewater icing.

◆ ◆ ◆

225 G/8 OZ PLAIN FLOUR

150 G/5 OZ BUTTER

100 G/4 OZ CASTER SUGAR

2.5 ML/$\frac{1}{2}$ TSP VANILLA ESSENCE

1 EGG, BEATEN

75 G/3 OZ GLACE CHERRIES, FINELY CHOPPED

175 G/6 OZ ICING SUGAR

15 ML/1 TBSP ROSEWATER

20-25 ML/4-5 TSP WATER

GLACE CHERRIES

MAKES 24

◆ ◆ ◆

Sift the flour into a bowl, add the butter and rub in until the mixture has a fine texture. Add the sugar. Stir in the essence with the egg and cherries and mix together to make a firm dough.

Knead lightly then take small pieces of dough and roll them into balls the size of a large pea. Arrange 8 balls in rings on greased baking sheets, pressing together slightly. Continue making rings until all the dough is used up. Bake at 190°C/375°F/Gas Mark 5 for 12-15 minutes. Cool for 2 minutes, then transfer to a wire rack to cool completely.

To make the icing, sift the icing sugar into a bowl, add the rosewater and enough water to make a smooth runny icing. Dip the tops of the biscuits into the icing then decorate each one with small pieces of cherry.

ORANGE MADELEINE COOKIES

A madeleine tin is ideal for this recipe, but if you don't have one, you can use a small-holed fancy bun tin instead.

◆ ◆ ◆

175 G/6 OZ UNSALTED BUTTER

75 G/3 OZ CASTER SUGAR

45 ML/3 TSP GRATED ORANGE RIND

150 G/5 OZ PLAIN FLOUR

50 G/2 OZ GROUND ALMONDS

50 G/2 OZ CORNFLOUR

CASTER SUGAR TO DUST

MAKES ABOUT 20

◆ ◆ ◆

Put the butter and sugar into a bowl and beat together until light and fluffy. Add the orange rind then sift in the flour, almonds and cornflour and mix together to form a soft paste.

The mixture may have to be cooked in two batches, depending on the size of the tin.

Press a little of the mixture into the well greased and floured moulds of the madeleine tin and smooth off the tops. Bake at 180°C/350°F/Gas Mark 4 for 15-20 minutes. Cool the cookies a little before carefully easing them out of the tin. Place on a wire rack, sprinkle with sugar and leave to cool completely.

TOP: *Orange Madeleine Cookies*
BOTTOM: *Cherry Garlands*

MARZIPAN LATTICE COOKIES

*For lovers of marzipan this
sandwiched biscuit will be a real treat.*

◆ ◆ ◆

225 G/8 OZ PLAIN FLOUR

2.5 ML/$\frac{1}{2}$ TSP BAKING POWDER

175 G/6 OZ UNSALTED BUTTER

100 G/4 OZ CASTER SUGAR

1 EGG YOLK

225 G/8 OZ MARZIPAN

45 ML/3 TBSP APRICOT JAM

150 G/5 0Z ICING SUGAR

YELLOW FOOD COLOURING

MAKES 20

◆ ◆ ◆

Sift the flour and baking powder into a bowl, add the
butter and rub in until the mixture has a fine texture.
Add the sugar and mix to a dough with the egg yolk.
Knead lightly until smooth then wrap and chill.

Roll out the dough thinly then cut into rounds or
ovals about 7.5 cm/3 inches in diameter and place on
greased baking sheets. Bake at 160°C/325°F/Gas Mark
3 for 15 minutes. Transfer to a wire rack to cool.

Roll out the marzipan thinly and cut out rounds
or ovals the same size as the biscuits. Spread half the
biscuits with jam, place marzipan on top then spread
with a little more jam and sandwich with the remaining
biscuits.

To make the icing, sift the icing sugar into a bowl and
mix with a little water and a few drops of yellow food
colouring to make a thick mixture. Place in a small
greaseproof paper bag and decorate each biscuit with
lattice patterned icing. Allow to set.

VIENNESE FINGERS

*An all-time favourite, these delicious
cookies are finished with chocolate. For a
less rich cookie, omit the chocolate
and dust with icing sugar.*

◆ ◆ ◆

225 G/8 OZ UNSALTED BUTTER, SOFTENED

60 G/2$\frac{1}{2}$ OZ ICING SUGAR

10 ML/2 TSP VANILLA ESSENCE

1 LARGE EGG, BEATEN

300 G/10 OZ PLAIN FLOUR

2.5 ML/$\frac{1}{2}$ TSP BAKING POWDER

225 G/8 OZ PLAIN CHOCOLATE

MAKES ABOUT 28

◆ ◆ ◆

Put the butter into a bowl with the icing sugar and beat
together until pale and soft. Beat in the vanilla essence
and egg. Sift in the flour and baking powder and mix
together to make a smooth dough.

Place the mixture in a piping bag fitted with a medium star nozzle and pipe finger shapes about 7.5 cm/3
inches long onto greased baking sheets. Bake at
190°C/375°F/Gas Mark 5 for 15-20 minutes until crisp
and pale golden. Transfer to a wire rack to cool.

To make the icing, break the chocolate into a bowl.
Stand the bowl over a pan of simmering water and stir
until the chocolate has melted.

Dip both ends of the cookies in the chocolate then
leave on a wire rack to set.

TOP: *Marzipan Lattice Cookies*
BOTTOM: *Viennese Fingers*

COFFEE DATE SWIRLS

A delicious little biscuit for afternoon tea.

◆ ◆ ◆

175 G/6 OZ UNSALTED BUTTER

50 G/2 OZ GOLDEN CASTER SUGAR

15 ML/1 TBSP INSTANT COFFEE DISSOLVED IN

5 ML/1 TSP HOT WATER

1 EGG, BEATEN

225 G/8 OZ PLAIN FLOUR

FILLING

225 G/8 OZ PITTED DATES, CHOPPED

150 ML/5 FL OZ WATER

15 ML/1 TBSP DARK RUM

50 G/2 OZ GROUND ALMONDS

MAKES ABOUT 36

◆ ◆ ◆

Put the butter and sugar into a bowl and beat together until pale and creamy. Add the dissolved coffee to the mixture with the egg and beat again. Sift in the flour then work together to make a stiff dough. Knead lightly until smooth then wrap and chill.

To make the filling, put the dates into a saucepan with the water and simmer for about 10 minutes until the dates are soft and the water has evaporated. Allow to cool then mash with a fork. Stir in the rum and ground almonds.

Roll out the dough to a rectangle about 23 x 32.5 cm/9 x 13 inches. Spread over the date mixture then roll up along the long side, Swiss-roll style. Wrap and chill until firm.

Cut 5 mm/$\frac{1}{4}$ inch slices and place on baking sheets lined with non-stick baking parchment. Bake at 180°C/350°F/Gas Mark 4 for 12-15 minutes.

FLORENTINES

Florentines are a rich mixture of nuts and fruits, coated on one side with chocolate.

◆ ◆ ◆

50 G/2 OZ BUTTER

75 G/3 OZ CASTER SUGAR

50 G/2 OZ BLANCHED ALMONDS, COARSELY CHOPPED

25 G/1 OZ HAZELNUTS, CHOPPED

25 G/1 OZ CRYSTALLISED GINGER, FINELY CHOPPED

50 G/2 OZ GLACE CHERRIES, CHOPPED

50 G/2 OZ MIXED PEEL

25 G/1 OZ PLAIN FLOUR

45 ML/3 TBSP SINGLE CREAM

175 G/6 OZ PLAIN CHOCOLATE

MAKES ABOUT 20

◆ ◆ ◆

Melt the butter in a saucepan then stir in the sugar and continue to stir over the heat until dissolved. Add the remaining ingredients except the chocolate.

Place dessertspoonfuls of the mixture onto greased baking sheets and flatten. Bake at 180°C/350°F/Gas Mark 4 for 10 minutes until golden. Use a palette knife and push in the ragged edges to neaten. Cool for 2 minutes then transfer to wire racks to cool completely.

Melt the chocolate in a bowl over a pan of simmering water. Spread over the undersides of the florentines. Allow the chocolate to set a little then make a wavy pattern with a fork. Leave to set.

TOP: *Florentines*
BOTTOM: *Coffee Date Swirls*

WALNUT CURLS

Although these biscuits are a bit fiddly to make, the mixture is simple and the result is elegant.

◆ ◆ ◆

50 G / 2 OZ BUTTER

100 G / 4 OZ CASTER SUGAR

2 EGG WHITES

40 G / 1 1/2 OZ PLAIN FLOUR

50 G / 2 OZ WALNUTS, VERY FINELY CHOPPED

MAKES 21

◆ ◆ ◆

Put the butter and sugar into a bowl and beat until light and creamy. Add the egg whites and beat until well combined but not frothy. Sift in the flour and fold it in with the nuts.

Drop teaspoonfuls of the mixture onto baking sheets lined with non-stick baking parchment and spread the batter into 5 cm/2 inch rounds. Bake at 180°C/ 350°F/Gas Mark 4 for 5-6 minutes, or until just turning golden round the edges.

Working quickly with each cookie, remove from the paper with a flat fish slice or palette knife, and roll, with the underside of the cookie inside, around pencils or chopsticks. Transfer to a wire rack to cool. If the cookies become too brittle to roll, return them to the oven for 30 seconds to soften.

BUTTERSCOTCH BISCUITS

Topping these biscuits with broken butterscotch sweets gives an interesting finish and delicious taste.

◆ ◆ ◆

100 G / 4 OZ SOFT MARGARINE

2.5 ML / 1/2 TSP VANILLA ESSENCE

40 G / 1 1/2 OZ LIGHT MUSCOVADO SUGAR, SIFTED

150 G / 5 OZ PLAIN FLOUR

25 G / 1 OZ CUSTARD POWDER

50 G / 2 OZ BUTTERSCOTCH SWEETS, ROUGHLY CRUSHED

MAKES 15

◆ ◆ ◆

Beat the margarine and sugar together until fluffy, add the vanilla essence then sift in the flour and mix to form a soft dough. Spoon into a piping bag fitted with a large star nozzle.

Pipe swirls onto greased baking sheets and top with the crushed butterscotch. Chill for 30 minutes.

Bake at 190°C/375°F/Gas Mark 5 for 10-12 minutes until pale golden. Cool slightly then transfer to a wire rack to cool completely.

TOP: *Walnut Curls*
BOTTOM: *Butterscotch Biscuits*

CHOCOLATE PISTACHIO FANCIES

Buy ready shelled pistachios for this recipe and make sure they are unsalted. The combination of the nuts and chocolate make these cookies a special treat.

◆ ◆ ◆

150 G/5 OZ BUTTER

2.5 ML/½ TSP VANILLA ESSENCE

75 G/3 OZ LIGHT MUSCOVADO SUGAR, SIFTED

75 G/3 OZ PISTACHIOS, CHOPPED

150 G/5 OZ PLAIN FLOUR

25 G/1 OZ COCOA

TOPPING

150 G/5 OZ MILK CHOCOLATE

25 G/1 OZ UNSALTED BUTTER

50 G/2 OZ PISTACHIOS, CHOPPED

MAKES 18

◆ ◆ ◆

Put the butter, vanilla essence and sugar into a bowl and beat until creamy. Add the nuts and sift in the flour and cocoa. Mix together to form a fairly stiff consistency.

Line a 23 cm/9 inch shallow square baking tin with non-stick baking parchment, then add the mixture. Flatten out evenly and bake at 190°C/375°F/Gas Mark 5 for 12-15 minutes. Allow to cool in the tin.

To make the topping, put the chocolate and butter into a bowl and place over a pan of simmering water. Stir until melted then spread over the biscuit base. Scatter over the chopped nuts and allow to set.

Cut into 9 squares then cut each square diagonally to give 18 triangles. Remove from the tin.

COCONUT TUILES

A simple mixture made to look impressive by curling the biscuits while still warm.

◆ ◆ ◆

2 EGG WHITES

100 G/4 OZ CASTER SUGAR

50 G/2 OZ UNSALTED BUTTER, MELTED

50 G/2 OZ PLAIN FLOUR

75 G/3 OZ DESICCATED COCONUT

MAKES ABOUT 18

◆ ◆ ◆

Whisk the egg whites until very frothy, fold in the sugar then the melted butter. Sift in the flour and add half the coconut. Use a large metal spoon to mix the ingredients together.

Line 2 baking sheets with non-stick paper. Spread dessertspoonfuls of the mixture onto the paper to form circles about 7.5 cm/3 inches in diameter. Sprinkle each with some of the remaining coconut and bake at 190°C/375°F/Gas Mark 5 for 5-6 minutes until golden.

Loosen the edges with a palette knife and lift each off with a flat fish slice. Place on a rolling pin and leave to cool. Do not cook too many at a time otherwise it will be difficult to shape them.

The non-stick paper can be turned and re-used to cook more biscuits.

TOP: *Coconut Tuiles*

BOTTOM: *Chocolate Pistachio Fancies*

CHOCOLATE MARZIPAN WHIRLS

An indulgent treat, these marzipan-flavoured biscuits are topped with a rich chocolate ganache. For extra flavour add a little amaretto liqueur to the topping mixture.

◆ ◆ ◆

100 G/4 OZ UNSALTED BUTTER

100 G/4 OZ MARZIPAN

FEW DROPS OF ALMOND ESSENCE

175 G/6 OZ PLAIN FLOUR

TOPPING

150 ML/5 FL OZ DOUBLE CREAM

300 G/10 OZ PLAIN CHOCOLATE

BLANCHED ALMONDS

MAKES ABOUT 24

◆ ◆ ◆

Put the butter and marzipan into a bowl and beat together until creamy. Add the almond essence and the flour then work together to make a smooth dough. Knead lightly then roll out to 5 mm/$\frac{1}{4}$ inch thick.

Use a 5 cm/2 inch cutter and cut out rounds, place them on greased baking sheets and chill for 30 minutes. Bake at 180°C/350°F/Gas Mark 4 for 10-12 minutes until golden. Transfer to a wire rack to cool.

Meanwhile, put the cream into a pan and heat to boiling point, remove from the heat and add the broken up chocolate. Stir until the chocolate melts and is smooth. Allow to cool then refrigerate until the mixture becomes thick enough to pipe.

Put the chocolate into a piping bag fitted with a star nozzle and pipe whirls on top of the biscuits. Decorate each biscuit with a blanched almond.

CRYSTALLISED GINGER CREAMS

The filling for these cookies uses crystallised ginger. If this is not available use stem ginger drained from its syrup or alternatively ginger marmalade.

◆ ◆ ◆

175 G/6 OZ UNSALTED BUTTER

50 G/2 OZ ICING SUGAR

175 G/6 OZ PLAIN FLOUR

50 G/2 OZ CUSTARD POWDER

10 ML/2 TSP GROUND GINGER

FILLING

75 G/3 OZ ICING SUGAR

25 G/1 OZ BUTTER

25 G/1 OZ CRYSTALLISED, GLACE, OR STEM

GINGER, FINELY CHOPPED

MAKES 16-18

◆ ◆ ◆

Put the butter and icing sugar into a bowl and beat together until creamy. Sift the flour with the custard powder and ginger and mix in to make a stiff dough.

Take pieces of the mixture and form into balls the size of a large walnut. Place on greased baking sheets then press down and flatten with a fork. Bake at 180°C/350°F/Gas Mark 4 for 10-12 minutes until golden. Transfer to a wire rack to cool.

To make the filling, put the icing sugar and butter into a bowl and beat together until creamy. Add the ginger and use to sandwich the biscuits together.

TOP: *Chocolate Marzipan Whirls*
BOTTOM: *Crystallized Ginger Creams*

NUTTY CRESCENTS

Many countries have recipes for crescent-shaped butter cookies with ground nuts and sugar. The Greeks have Kourambiedes and the Viennese Kupferlin.

◆ ◆ ◆

225 G/8 OZ UNSALTED BUTTER
100 G/4 OZ CASTER SUGAR
300 G/10 OZ PLAIN FLOUR
175 G/6 OZ LIGHTLY TOASTED HAZELNUTS,
GROUND
2.5 ML/$\frac{1}{2}$ TSP VANILLA ESSENCE
ICING SUGAR TO DUST

MAKES ABOUT 30

◆ ◆ ◆

Put the butter into a bowl with the sugar and sift in the flour. Rub in until the mixture resembles very fine crumbs. Add the nuts and vanilla essence and mix together until the dough is smooth.

Take small pieces of dough and roll into 10 cm/4 inch lengths. Shape into small crescents and place on greased baking sheets. Bake at 180°C/350°F/Gas Mark 4 for 10-15 minutes until golden.

Transfer to a wire rack to cool then dust liberally with icing sugar.

IRISH LACE COOKIES

These attractive cookies are quite delicate and require careful handling.

◆ ◆ ◆

100 G/4 OZ BUTTER
75 G/3 OZ LIGHT MUSCOVADO SUGAR, SIFTED
30 ML/2 TBSP GOLDEN SYRUP
25 G/1 OZ PLAIN FLOUR
75 G/3 OZ ROLLED OATS
5 ML/1 TSP VANILLA ESSENCE
30 ML/2 TBSP MILK

MAKES 25

◆ ◆ ◆

Melt the butter in a saucepan then stir in the sugar and golden syrup. Add the remaining ingredients and mix again. Drop rounded teaspoonfuls of the mixture onto greased baking sheets and bake at 180°C/350°F/Gas Mark 4 for 8-9 minutes until golden brown.

Cool for just 1 minute then carefully remove with a spatula and place on a rolling pin to cool. If the cookies become brittle return them to the oven for 30 seconds to soften. Do not cook too many at once, otherwise it will be difficult to shape them. Once the cookies have cooled in shape, transfer them to a wire rack to cool completely.

TOP: *Nutty Crescents*
BOTTOM: *Irish Lace Cookies*

COFFEE CREAM CRUMBLES

These cookies can be made and stored in advance, but only sandwich them together on the day of eating. Perfect for a special afternoon tea.

◆ ◆ ◆

225 G/8 OZ UNSALTED BUTTER
100 G/4 OZ ICING SUGAR
20 ML/4 TSP INSTANT COFFEE DISSOLVED IN
15 ML/1 TBSP HOT WATER
350 G/12 OZ PLAIN FLOUR

FILLING

175 G/6 OZ ICING SUGAR
50 G/2 OZ UNSALTED BUTTER
30 ML/2 TBSP SINGLE CREAM
ICING SUGAR TO DUST

M A K E S   A B O U T   2 0

◆ ◆ ◆

Put the butter and icing sugar into a bowl and beat together until light and creamy. Add the dissolved coffee to the mixture. Sift in the flour and work together to make a soft dough.

Place the dough in a piping bag fitted with a star nozzle and pipe out stars onto greased baking sheets. Bake at 180°C/350°F/Gas Mark 4 for 10-12 minutes. Transfer to a wire rack to cool.

To make the buttercream filling, beat together the ingredients until creamy (but do not overbeat). Place the buttercream in a small piping bag fitted with a small star nozzle and pipe a swirl on half of the cookies. Sandwich with the remaining cookies and dust the tops with icing sugar.

APRICOT ALMANDINES

Use a good-quality apricot jam for these biscuits. Do not keep them any longer than 2 days as they will soften.

◆ ◆ ◆

225 G/8 OZ PLAIN FLOUR
75 G/3 OZ ICING SUGAR
175 G/6 OZ UNSALTED BUTTER
100 G/4 OZ GROUND ALMONDS
5 ML/1 TSP ALMOND ESSENCE
1 EGG, SEPARATED
50 G/2 OZ BLANCHED ALMONDS, CHOPPED
60 ML/4 TBSP APRICOT JAM

M A K E S   2 8

◆ ◆ ◆

Sift the flour and icing sugar into a bowl, add the butter and rub in to make a fine textured mixture. Stir in the ground almonds then mix to a dough with the almond essence and egg yolk. Knead until smooth, then wrap and chill for 30 minutes.

Roll out the dough thinly to about 3 mm/1/8th inch then cut out small rounds with a 5 cm/2 inch fancy cutter. Cut out the centres from half and place on greased baking sheets. Brush the rings with egg white, and sprinkle with the chopped almonds. Bake at 190°C/375°F/Gas Mark 5 for 10-12 minutes until golden. Transfer to a wire rack to cool.

Spread the rounds with jam and cover with the almond-covered rings.

TOP: *Coffee Cream Crumbles*
BOTTOM: *Apricot Almandines*

MOCHA SLICES

◆ ◆ ◆

150 G/5 OZ BUTTER

50 G/2 OZ LIGHT MUSCOVADO SUGAR, SIFTED

1 EGG, BEATEN

175 G/6 OZ SELF-RAISING FLOUR

15 ML/1 TBSP COCOA

MOCHA CREAM

50 G/2 OZ UNSALTED BUTTER

150 G/5 OZ ICING SUGAR

10 ML/2 TSP INSTANT COFFEE DISSOLVED IN

5 ML/1 TSP HOT WATER

50 G/2 OZ PLAIN CHOCOLATE, MELTED

ICING

175 G/6 OZ ICING SUGAR, SIFTED

10 ML/2 TSP INSTANT COFFEE DISSOLVED IN

20 ML/4 TSP HOT WATER

40 G/1$\frac{1}{2}$ OZ PLAIN CHOCOLATE, MELTED

MAKES 14 SLICES

◆ ◆ ◆

Cream the butter and sugar until fluffy, add the egg and beat again. Sift in the flour and cocoa and beat until smooth. Press evenly into a lined 23 x 33 cm/9 x 13 inch Swiss roll tin. Bake at 180°C/350°F/Gas Mark 4 for 12-15 minutes. Invert onto a wire rack and peel away the paper. Cut the pastry in half across the middle.

Put all the ingredients for the mocha cream into a bowl and beat together until smooth. Spread over one half of the pastry, then sandwich the other on top.

Add the dissolved coffee to the icing sugar and mix until smooth. Spread over the top of the pastry. Quickly pipe lines of chocolate across the icing then draw a skewer through to give a feather effect. Allow to set before cutting into fingers.

PECAN AND MAPLE HEARTS

A delicious combination of flavours, these biscuits would make a special gift for friends or family.

◆ ◆ ◆

175 G/6 OZ UNSALTED BUTTER

75 G/3 OZ LIGHT MUSCOVADO SUGAR, SIFTED

250 G/9 OZ PLAIN FLOUR

75 G/3 OZ PECANS, FINELY CHOPPED

FILLING

175 G/6 OZ ICING SUGAR

50 G/2 OZ BUTTER

45 ML/3 TBSP MAPLE SYRUP

ICING SUGAR TO DUST

MAKES 20

◆ ◆ ◆

Put the butter and sugar into a bowl and beat together until creamy. Stir in the flour and nuts and work together to make a smooth dough. Knead lightly, then wrap and chill for 30 minutes.

Roll out thinly, and using a medium-sized heart-shaped cutter, cut out the biscuits. Place on greased baking sheets and bake at 190°C/375°F/Gas Mark 5 for 8-10 minutes. Transfer to a wire rack to cool.

To make the filling, beat the icing sugar and butter together. Beat in the maple syrup, then spread over half of the biscuits. Sandwich with the remaining biscuits and dust with icing sugar.

TOP: *Pecan and Maple Hearts*
BOTTOM: *Mocha Slices*

TRAY BAKES

The cookies in this chapter are all baked in a large block, cooled, then cut into squares, bars, fingers, triangles or diamonds. They are easy to make as they do not require special shaping. Often moist and chewy, they are an excellent standby for hungry children and with the addition of high-fibre ingredients they make healthy snacks for lunch-boxes or picnics.

A variety of shallow baking tins have been used in these recipes. Most kitchens have a Swiss roll tin, but do try to use a tin with the measurements specified in each recipe, as the quantity of ingredients has been calculated for the size recommended.

In some recipes it is suggested that the tin is lined; this will help ease out the cookies after baking. Tray-baked cookies are cooled in the tin before being cut into shapes.

Most cookies can be frozen successfully either in their raw state or after baking; it is better to freeze baked cookies undecorated. Open-freeze cookies until solid then pack in rigid containers for storage. Cover and label the container and store for up to two months. Freezing cookies means you can always offer homemade treats when unexpected visitors arrive. Thaw baked cookies for about 15 minutes at room temperature. Unbaked piped, shaped or tray-baked cookies can be baked without thawing; simply follow the recipe and add a few minutes to the baking time.

CONTENTS

◆ ◆ ◆

Strawberry Linzer Bars
Date Butter Cookies   *56*

Poppyseed Apricot Cookies
Chocolate Pecan Bars   *58*

Figgy Rolls
Marmalade Crunchies   *60*

Chocolate Caramels
Hazelnut Flapjacks   *62*

Tutti-Frutti Squares
Dutch Cinnamon Biscuits   *64*

Cherry Almond Bakewells
Nutty Honey Diamonds   *66*

Coconut Squares
Sesame Triangles   *68*

Apple Cinnamon Crumbles
Glazed Lemon Shorties   *70*

STRAWBERRY LINZER BARS

Adapted from the Viennese dessert, Linzertorte, these cookies can be made with your favourite jam. Use a good-quality preserve with a high proportion of fruit.

◆ ◆ ◆

175 G/6 OZ BUTTER

225 G/8 OZ CASTER SUGAR

1 EGG, BEATEN

GRATED RIND OF 1 LEMON

225 G/8 OZ PLAIN FLOUR

5 ML/1 TSP GROUND CINNAMON

100 G/4 OZ GROUND ALMONDS

300 G/10 OZ STRAWBERRY CONSERVE

ICING SUGAR TO DUST

MAKES 24

◆ ◆ ◆

In a bowl beat the butter and sugar together until light and creamy. Beat in the egg and lemon rind. Sift the flour and cinnamon together then add to the mixture with the ground almonds to make a dough.

Turn onto a floured surface and knead lightly, wrap in cling-film and refrigerate for 30 minutes.

Take two-thirds of the dough and press into a greased 23 x 33 cm/9 x 13 inch Swiss roll tin. Spread over the conserve.

With floured hands, take small pieces of the remaining dough and roll into pencil-thin strips. Arrange the strips over the jam in a lattice pattern. Chill for 30 minutes.

Bake at 180°C/350°F/Gas Mark 4 for about 35-40 minutes until golden and cooked through. Allow to cool in the tin. Dust with icing sugar then cut into bars.

DATE BUTTER COOKIES

Do not use ready-chopped, sugar-coated dates or any with a sticky coating for this recipe or it will be too sweet.

◆ ◆ ◆

175 G/6 OZ BUTTER

75 G/3 OZ GOLDEN CASTER SUGAR

175 G/6 OZ SELF-RAISING FLOUR

50 G/2 OZ GROUND RICE

175 G/6 OZ STONED DATES, CHOPPED

MAKES 16

◆ ◆ ◆

Cream the butter and sugar together until light and fluffy. Stir in the rest of the ingredients and mix well.

Turn the mixture into a greased shallow tin 18 x 28 cm/7 x 11 inches. Level the surface and prick all over with a fork.

Bake at 180°C/350°F/Gas Mark 4 for 10 minutes. Mark into fingers then return to the oven and cook a further 10 minutes until golden.

Allow to cool in the tin. With a sharp knife cut through again into fingers and remove from the tin.

LEFT: *Date Butter Cookies*
RIGHT: *Strawberry Linzer Bars*

POPPYSEED APRICOT COOKIES

The apricots add a delicious tang to these cookies. Ready-to-eat fruit needs no soaking.

◆ ◆ ◆

100 G/4 OZ READY-TO-EAT DRIED APRICOTS

100 G/4 OZ GOLDEN GRANULATED SUGAR

175 G/6 OZ BUTTER OR MARGARINE

1 LARGE EGG, BEATEN

15 ML/1 TBSP LEMON JUICE

350 G/12 OZ SELF-RAISING FLOUR

30 ML/2 TBSP POPPYSEEDS

100 G/4 OZ ICING SUGAR

MAKES ABOUT 24

◆ ◆ ◆

Place the apricots in a pan with 25 g/1 oz of the sugar and 60 ml/4 tbsp water. Simmer for 5 minutes. Cool slightly, then work to a rough textured purée in a blender or food processor.

Put the butter or margarine into a bowl with the remaining granulated sugar and beat until light and fluffy. Add the egg and lemon juice, then add the flour and poppyseeds and mix to a softish dough.

Divide the dough into three pieces. Roll each to a rope about 25 cm/10 inches long, then pat out to make a rectangle 5 cm/2 inches wide. Press down the middle to make a channel, spread the apricot purée down the middle of each. Transfer to greased baking sheets and bake at 180°C/350°F/Gas Mark 4 for 18-20 minutes.

Mix the icing sugar with a little water to make a thin icing, then drizzle from a spoon over the cooled cookies and allow to set. Cut the logs into slices.

CHOCOLATE PECAN BARS

A wonderful combination of chocolate and nuts, this will not last long enough to be stored in the cookie tin.

◆ ◆ ◆

100 G/4 OZ BUTTER

175 G/6 OZ PLAIN FLOUR

TOPPING

50 G/2 OZ BUTTER

100 G/4 OZ PLAIN CHOCOLATE

100 G/4 OZ GOLDEN SYRUP

100 G/4 OZ DARK MUSCOVADO SUGAR

2.5 ML/$\frac{1}{2}$ TSP VANILLA ESSENCE

3 EGGS, BEATEN

175 G/6 OZ PECAN NUTS, ROUGHLY CHOPPED

MAKES 24

◆ ◆ ◆

Rub the butter into the flour and bind together with cold water to make a pastry dough. Use to line a Swiss roll tin 20 x 30 cm/8 x 12 inches. Trim the edges.

Melt the butter and chocolate in a bowl over a pan of simmering water. Put the syrup, sugar, vanilla essence and eggs into a large bowl and whisk until light and frothy, then whisk in the melted mixture. Pour over the pastry and scatter over the nuts.

Bake at 180°C/350°F/Gas Mark 4 for about 50 minutes until the filling feels firm. Allow to cool in the tin then cut into bars 4 x 7.5 cm/1$\frac{1}{2}$ x 3 inches.

TOP: *Poppyseed Apricot Cookies*
BOTTOM: *Chocolate Pecan Bars*

FIGGY ROLLS

*These cookies with a hint of orange
are really tasty.*

◆ ◆ ◆

225 G/8 OZ SELF-RAISING FLOUR

5 ML/1 TSP MIXED SPICE

50 G/2 OZ LIGHT MUSCOVADO SUGAR, SIFTED

100 G/4 OZ UNSALTED BUTTER

1 EGG. BEATEN

FILLING

225 G/8 OZ READY-TO-EAT DRIED FIGS

50 G/2 OZ DARK MUSCOVADO SUGAR

GRATED RIND AND JUICE OF 1 LARGE ORANGE

50 G/2 OZ DRY SPONGE FINGERS, CRUSHED

TOPPING

MILK

GOLDEN GRANUALTED SUGAR

M A K E S   3 0

◆ ◆ ◆

Sift the flour and spice into a bowl. Rub in the butter then add the sugar and egg. Mix to a dough then knead until smooth. Wrap and refrigerate.

Place the figs in a saucepan with 150 ml/5 fl oz water and simmer for 10 minutes. Add the sugar and orange rind and juice, and simmer until most of the liquid has evaporated. Purée then allow to cool. Stir in the crumbs.

Divide the dough into 2 and roll out each piece to 10 x 30 cm/6 x 12 inches. Place half the fig mixture down the centre of each strip, dampen the edges with a little milk, then roll up. Place on a greased baking sheet with the joins underneath. Brush with milk and sprinkle with sugar. Bake at 190°C/ 375°F/Gas Mark 5 for 20 minutes. When cold cut each roll into 15 slices.

MARMALADE CRUNCHIES

*Another wholesome treat
to offer children after school.*

◆ ◆ ◆

225 G/8 OZ CRUNCHY OAT CEREAL

50 G/2 OZ CHOPPED MIXED NUTS

100 G/4 OZ WHOLEMEAL SELF-RAISING

FLOUR

175 G/6 OZ MARGARINE

30 ML/2 TBSP GOLDEN SYRUP

75 ML/5 TBSP COARSE-CUT SEVILLE ORANGE

MARMALADE

M A K E S   1 6

◆ ◆ ◆

Put the crunchy oat cereal into a polythene bag and crush with a rolling pin. Tip into a bowl and mix with the nuts and flour.

Melt the margarine with the golden syrup, then pour onto the dry ingredients and mix together. Press half of the mixture into the base of a greased 20 cm/8 inch shallow square tin. Spread over the marmalade then top with the remaining oat mixture, pressing down gently.

Bake at 180°C/350°F/Gas Mark 4 for 25 minutes. Cool slightly then mark into small squares. Leave in the tin to cool. Use a sharp knife to cut up the squares.

TOP: *Figgy Rolls*
BOTTOM: *Marmalade Crunchies*

CHOCOLATE CARAMELS

*A very sweet cookie, but a very
popular one too!*

◆ ◆ ◆

100 G/4 OZ BUTTER

175 G/6 OZ PLAIN FLOUR

50 G/2 OZ GOLDEN CASTER SUGAR

FILLING

175 G/6 OZ BUTTER

100 G/4 OZ GOLDEN CASTER SUGAR

45 ML/3 TBSP GOLDEN SYRUP

397 G/14 OZ CAN CONDENSED SKIMMED

MILK

TOPPING

175 G/6 OZ PLAIN CHOCOLATE

25 G/1 OZ UNSALTED BUTTER

MAKES 24

◆ ◆ ◆

Line a 23 cm/9 inch shallow square tin with non-stick
baking parchment. Rub the butter into the flour, stir in
the sugar then turn into the prepared tin and press
down. Bake at 180°C/350°F/Gas Mark 4 for 20-25
minutes until golden.

Meanwhile, put the filling ingredients into a saucepan
and melt over a low heat. When all the sugar has dissolved, bring to the boil and simmer for 6-8 minutes,
stirring all the time until it becomes very thick. Pour
over the base and refrigerate until firm.

Melt the chocolate and butter together, mix until
smooth and allow to cool. Spread over the caramel then
chill again until set. With a sharp knife, cut into pieces
about 4 x 5 cm/1$\frac{1}{2}$ x 2 inches.

HAZELNUT FLAPJACKS

*Very quick and easy to make, these flapjacks
are an ideal treat for children's lunch boxes
or after-school snack.*

◆ ◆ ◆

200 G/7 OZ ROLLED OATS

100 G/4 OZ HAZELNUTS, LIGHTLY TOASTED

AND CHOPPED

50 G/2 OZ WHOLEMEAL PLAIN FLOUR

100 G/4 OZ BUTTER OR MARGARINE

30 ML/2 TBSP CLEAR HONEY

75 G/3 OZ LIGHT MUSCOVADO SUGAR

MAKES 16 PIECES

◆ ◆ ◆

Put the oats, hazelnuts and flour into a large bowl and
mix together. In a saucepan heat the butter or margarine with the honey and sugar until melted. Pour
onto the dry ingredients and mix well.

Turn into a greased 23 cm/9 inch square shallow tin
and level, pressing down with the back of a spoon.

Bake at 180°C/350°F/Gas Mark 4 for 20-25 minutes
until golden and firm to the touch. Mark into 12 or 24
pieces and allow to cool in the tin. Cut through with a
sharp knife and remove.

TOP: *Chocolate Caramels*
BOTTOM: *Hazelnut Flapjacks*

TUTTI FRUTTI SQUARES

Packed with delicious fruit, these cookies will appeal to all ages – perfect for packed lunches and picnics.

◆ ◆ ◆

100 G/4 OZ WHOLEMEAL SELF-RAISING FLOUR

100 G/4 OZ LIGHT MUSCOVADO SUGAR

50 G/2 OZ BUTTER OR MARGARINE

T O P P I N G

100 G/4 OZ SULTANAS

50 G/2 OZ DESICCATED COCONUT

75 G/3 OZ GLACE CHERRIES, CHOPPED

50 G/2 OZ MIXED CANDIED PEEL

2 EGGS, BEATEN

50 G/2 OZ LIGHT MUSCOVADO SUGAR

50 G/2 OZ WHOLEMEAL SELF-RAISING FLOUR

M A K E S   1 5

◆ ◆ ◆

Sift the flour and sugar together into a bowl. Add the butter or margarine and rub in to resemble fine crumbs.

Turn into a greased 18 x 28 cm/7 x 11 inch shallow baking tin and press down evenly. Bake at 170°C/325°F/Gas Mark 3 for 10-12 minutes until light golden. Remove from the oven.

Meanwhile, put all the topping ingredients into a bowl and mix together. Spread evenly over the shortbread base and return to the oven to bake for 30 minutes.

Cool slightly before marking into squares. Leave in the tin until cold before cutting up.

DUTCH CINNAMON BISCUITS

The Dutch are very fond of their cookies and morning coffee and afternoon tea are always accompanied by something from the local bakery. Some Dutch towns have been famous for hundreds of years for their particular specialities made with butter and spices.

◆ ◆ ◆

225 G/8 OZ PLAIN FLOUR

7.5ML/1$\frac{1}{2}$ TSP GROUND CINNAMON

100 G/4 OZ UNSALTED BUTTER

75 G/3 OZ GOLDEN CASTER SUGAR

M A K E S   1 6

◆ ◆ ◆

Sift the flour and cinnamon into a bowl, rub in the butter until the mixture resembles fine crumbs. Stir in the sugar then turn into a lightly greased 18 x 28 cm/7 x 11 inch shallow baking tin. Press the mixture evenly into the tin then rough up the surface with a fork. Chill for 1 hour.

Bake at 180°C/350°F/Gas Mark 4 for 20-25 minutes until golden. While still hot use a sharp knife and cut into 16 bars.

TOP: *Tutti Frutti Squares*

BOTTOM: *Dutch Cinnamon Biscuits*

CHERRY ALMOND BAKEWELLS

A super recipe for a special weekend tea.

◆ ◆ ◆

100 G/4 OZ BUTTER OR MARGARINE

175 G/6 OZ PLAIN FLOUR

25 G/1 OZ CASTER SUGAR

60-75 ML/4-5 TBSP CHERRY JAM

TOPPING

100 G/4 OZ SOFT MARGARINE

100 G/4 OZ GOLDEN CASTER SUGAR

2 EGGS

75 G/3 OZ SELF-RAISING FLOUR

75 G/3 OZ GROUND ALMONDS

2.5 ML/$^1/_2$ TSP ALMOND ESSENCE

50 G/2 OZ FLAKED ALMONDS

ICING

15 G/$^1/_2$ OZ UNSALTED BUTTER

150 G/5 OZ ICING SUGAR

15-30 ML/1-2 TBSP LEMON JUICE

MAKES 24

◆ ◆ ◆

Rub the butter or margarine into the flour, add the sugar then mix with a little cold water to make a pastry dough. Knead lightly then roll out and line a Swiss roll tin 20 x 30 cm/8 x 12 inches. Spread over the jam.

Put the topping ingredients into a bowl and beat for 2 minutes then spoon onto the jam and level the surface. Scatter over the flaked almonds then bake at 180°C/350°F/Gas Mark 4 for 25-30 minutes until golden.

Beat the remaining butter and icing sugar with enough lemon juice to make a thick icing. Place in a small greaseproof paper bag and drizzle over the cooled tray bake. Allow to set then cut into bars.

NUTTY HONEY DIAMONDS

*For anyone who likes nuts,
this will be a winner.*

◆ ◆ ◆

100 G/4 OZ MARGARINE

75 G/3 OZ GOLDEN CASTER SUGAR

1 EGG, BEATEN

175 G/6 OZ WHOLEMEAL SELF-RAISING
FLOUR

TOPPING

100 G/4 OZ WALNUTS, FINELY CHOPPED

100 G/4 OZ WHOLE ALMONDS, CHOPPED

90 ML/6 TBSP CLEAR HONEY

2 EGGS, BEATEN

WALNUT HALVES TO DECORATE

MAKES 16

◆ ◆ ◆

Cream the margarine and sugar together until light and fluffy. Add the egg then the flour and mix to make a dough. Press into the base of a greased oblong shallow tin, 22 x 29 cm/8$^1/_2$ x 11$^1/_2$ inches and bake at 180°C/350°F/Gas Mark 4 for 10-12 minutes until golden.

To make the topping, combine the nuts with half of the honey and the eggs. Spoon over the base and return to the oven for 15-20 minutes until richly golden.

Brush the remaining honey over the top. Cut into diamonds (there will be some small triangles left in the corners) and decorate each with a walnut half. Cool in the tin before removing.

TOP: *Nutty Honey Diamonds*
BOTTOM: *Cherry Almond Bakewells*

COCONUT SQUARES

Take care not to overcook these delicious cookies, otherwise the coconut topping will harden and lose its moist texture.

◆ ◆ ◆

100 G/4 OZ BUTTER OR MARGARINE

75 G/3 OZ GOLDEN CASTER SUGAR

2 EGG YOLKS

175 G/6 OZ SELF-RAISING FLOUR

50 G/2 OZ DESICCATED COCONUT

90 ML/6 TBSP RASPBERRY JAM, WARMED

T O P P I N G

3 EGG WHITES

175 G/6 OZ ICING SUGAR

175 G/6 OZ DESICCATED COCONUT

M A K E S   2 8

◆ ◆ ◆

Beat the butter or margarine with the sugar until creamy, add the egg yolks and beat again. Stir in the flour and coconut and mix together. Press into the base of a greased oblong shallow tin 22 x 29 cm/8½ x 11½ inches. Bake at 180°C/350°F/Gas Mark 4 for 10 minutes.

Spread the jam over the base. Whisk the egg whites until stiff, fold in the icing sugar and coconut, then spoon over the jam. Gently level out with a fork and return to the oven at 300°C/150°F/Gas Mark 2 for 30-40 minutes until light golden. Cool in the tin then cut into squares.

SESAME TRIANGLES

A thin cookie packed with lots of flavour and goodness.

◆ ◆ ◆

175 G/6 OZ MEDIUM OATMEAL

75 G/3 OZ SESAME SEEDS, LIGHTLY ROASTED

50 G/2 OZ LIGHT MUSCOVADO SUGAR, SIFTED

60 ML/4 TBSP CLEAR HONEY

75 ML/5 TBSP SUNFLOWER OIL

M A K E S   2 4

◆ ◆ ◆

Put the dry ingredients into a bowl and mix together. Add the honey and oil and mix again.

Line a 20 x 30 cm/8 x 12 inch Swiss roll tin with non-stick baking parchment, then turn the mixture into the tin. Level with a palette knife and bake at 180°C/350°F/Gas Mark 4 for 20-25 minutes.

Cool for 2 minutes then cut into 12 squares and across into triangles. Allow to cool completely before removing from the paper.

TOP: *Coconut Squares*
BOTTOM: *Sesame Triangles*

APPLE CINNAMON CRUMBLES

These are best eaten the same day, because the apple filling will make them soft if kept.

◆ ◆ ◆

100 G/4 OZ SELF-RAISING FLOUR

100 G/4 OZ PLAIN FLOUR

15 ML/1 TBSP GROUND CINNAMON

75 G/3 OZ ICING SUGAR

75 G/3 OZ GROUND ALMONDS

175 G/6 OZ BUTTER

1 EGG, BEATEN

450 G/1 LB BRAMLEY COOKING APPLES

45 ML/3 TBSP GOLDEN GRANULATED SUGAR

MAKES 32

◆ ◆ ◆

Sift the flours with 10 ml/2 tsp of cinnamon and icing sugar. Add the ground almonds then rub in the butter. Mix to a dough with the egg, turn onto a floured surface and knead until smooth.

Take one-third of the dough, wrap and freeze it until hard. Press the remaining dough into a greased Swiss roll tin 20 x 30 cm/8 x 12 inches and refrigerate.

Bake the dough in the tin for 10 minutes at 180°C/350°F/Gas Mark 4. Grate the apples with the skin on. Mix with 30 ml/2 tbsp of the sugar and spread over the base. Coarsely grate the frozen dough and scatter over the apple. Mix the remaining cinnamon and sugar together, sprinkle on top, then bake for a further 25 minutes. Cut into 32 pieces when cold.

GLAZED LEMON SHORTIES

A delicious variation on shortbread.

◆ ◆ ◆

175 G/6 OZ UNSALTED BUTTER, SOFTENED

50 G/2 OZ CASTER SUGAR

15 ML/1 TBSP GRATED LEMON RIND

15 ML/1 TBSP LEMON JUICE

225 G/8 OZ PLAIN FLOUR

50 G/2 OZ GROUND RICE

GLAZE

50 G/2 OZ ICING SUGAR

15 ML/1 TBSP LEMON JUICE

MAKES 24

◆ ◆ ◆

Cream the butter and sugar together until light and fluffy, add the lemon rind and juice and beat again.

Fold in the flour and ground rice and mix well to form a firm dough. Knead lightly until smooth, then cut the dough in half.

Roll out each piece to a rectangle 7.5 x 30 cm/3 x 12 inches and place on greased baking sheets. Chill for 30 minutes.

Bake at 180°C/350°F/Gas Mark 4 for 25-30 minutes until golden. Mix the icing sugar with the lemon juice and brush over the shortbread. With a sharp knife cut into wedges and transfer to a wire rack to cool.

TOP: *Glazed Lemon Shorties*
BOTTOM: *Apple Cinnamon Crumbles*

FESTIVE COOKIES

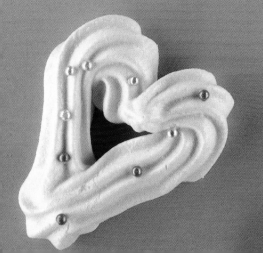

Throughout the seasons and in every country there are cookies or biscuits traditionally baked for special occasions. They are often associated with religious festivals, for example, or the recipe may be based simply on an ingredient plentiful in that part of the world. They are all variations on a basic mixture; it is the shape or decoration which gives them their special significance.

Although many cookies can be stored for two or three weeks in airtight containers, they do tend to dry out and lose the delicious flavour of freshly baked cookies. For ideal storing, line the bottom of the container with greaseproof paper and place another sheet of paper between each two layers of cookies or between each single layer of soft ones. Store different types of cookies in separate containers. Cookies filled with jam or buttercream should be eaten soon after filling. If you want to make them ahead of time, you can bake cookies and fill or decorate them shortly before serving. Should plain cookies lose their crispness during storage, return them to the oven at 160°C/325°F/Gas Mark 3 for about 5 minutes.

If you are making cookies to give away, encourage the recipient to eat them as soon as possible while they are still fresh. Cookies that are hung on Christmas trees should not be left too long before eating as they will become stale; allow the children to eat them daily and replace them from the cookie tin.

CONTENTS

◆ ◆ ◆

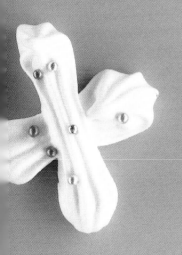

Valentine Knots
Meringue Hearts and Kisses   *74*

Poppyseed Pouches
Cream Cheese Cookies   *76*

Easter Currant Cookies
Festive Orange Biscuits   *78*

Highland Shortbread
Christmas Fruit and Nut Cookies   *80*

Lebkuchen
Cane Cookies   *82*

Cinnamon Stars
Festive Spicy Twists   *84*

VALENTINE KNOTS

A lovely combination of chocolate and walnut flavours to make very pretty shaped cookies.

◆ ◆ ◆

175 G/6 OZ BUTTER

100 G/4 OZ CASTER SUGAR

30 ML/2 TBSP BRANDY

FEW DROPS OF VANILLA ESSENCE

250 G/9 OZ PLAIN FLOUR

25 G/1 OZ PLAIN CHOCOLATE, FINELY GRATED

25 G/1 OZ WALNUTS, FINELY CHOPPED

MAKES 27

◆ ◆ ◆

Put the butter and sugar into a bowl and beat until light and fluffy, add the brandy and vanilla essence. Sift in the flour then mix until the crumbly stage is reached. Divide the mixture into two, add the chocolate to one and the walnuts to the other. Work each together to make a smooth dough then wrap and chill for 30 minutes.

Divide each piece of dough into 27 small balls. Take one of each flavour and roll out into a thin ropes about 12.5 cm/5 inches long using your fingers, then twist them together, form into a circle and pinch the ends together. Place on a greased baking sheet. Repeat with the remaining dough. Bake at 180°C/350°F/Gas Mark 4 for 12-15 minutes. Transfer to a wire rack to cool.

MERINGUE HEARTS AND KISSES

A fun way of making meringues. Colour some of the mixture with pink food colouring if wished.

◆ ◆ ◆

3 EGG WHITES

175 G/6 OZ CASTER SUGAR

COLOURED SUGAR BALLS TO DECORATE

MAKES ABOUT 20

◆ ◆ ◆

Put the egg whites into a clean bowl and whisk until stiff and dry. Gradually whisk in half the sugar, keeping the mixture stiff and glossy. Carefully fold in the remaining sugar. Place the meringue in a piping bag fitted with a 2.5 cm/$\frac{1}{2}$ inch star nozzle and pipe hearts and kisses onto baking sheets lined with non-stick paper. Scatter over coloured sugar balls for decoration.

Bake at 130°C/250°F/Gas Mark $\frac{1}{2}$ for about 1 hour or until crisp. When cool, peel off the lining paper.

TOP: *Valentine Knots*

BOTTOM: *Meringue Hearts and Kisses*

POPPYSEED POUCHES

These pastries, Hamentaschen, are traditional for the Jewish festival of Purim.

◆ ◆ ◆

150 G/5 OZ BUTTER OR MARGARINE

100 G/4 OZ CASTER SUGAR

1 EGG, BEATEN

FEW DROPS OF VANILLA ESSENCE

300 G/10 OZ PLAIN FLOUR

5 ML/1 TSP BAKING POWDER

100 G/4 OZ CASTER SUGAR

100 G/4 OZ POPPYSEEDS

15 ML/1 TBSP HONEY

GRATED RIND AND JUICE OF 1/2 LEMON

2.5 ML/1/2 TSP CINNAMON

50 G/2 OZ RAISINS, CHOPPED

25 G/1 OZ ALMONDS, FINELY CHOPPED

1 SMALL EGG, BEATEN

MAKES 30-36

◆ ◆ ◆

Beat the butter and sugar until fluffy, beat in the egg and essence. Sift in the flour and baking powder and mix to form a dough. Knead lightly then wrap and chill.

Heat the sugar with 60 ml/2 fl oz water until dissolved then bring to the boil. Add the poppy seeds, honey, lemon rind and juice and cinnamon. Bring back to the boil, stirring. Add the raisins, nuts and egg. Cool.

Roll out the dough to 3 mm/1/8th inch and cut out 7.5 cm/3 inch rounds with a fluted cutter. Put a teaspoon of filling in the centre of each, brush edges with water, then bring them to the centre to form a tricorn. Place on greased baking sheets and chill for 30 minutes. Bake at 180°C/350°F/Gas Mark 4 for 15-20 minutes.

CREAM CHEESE COOKIES

These cinnamon and walnut filled cookies are also known as Rugelach. The pastry is made with cream cheese and is popular in Israel.

◆ ◆ ◆

100 G/4 OZ BUTTER

100 G/4 OZ CREAM CHEESE

10 ML/2 TSP LEMON JUICE

225 G/8 OZ PLAIN FLOUR

2 EGG YOLKS

FILLING

50 G/2 OZ LIGHT MUSCOVADO SUGAR

5 ML/1 TSP GROUND CINNAMON

75 G/3 OZ RAISINS, CHOPPED

100 G/4 OZ WALNUTS, FINELY CHOPPED

TO DECORATE

GRANULATED SUGAR

MAKES 28

◆ ◆ ◆

Put the butter and cream cheese into a bowl and beat together until creamy. Add the lemon juice and then the flour and egg yolks and mix to form a smooth dough. Knead lightly then wrap and chill for 30 minutes.

Mix ingredients for the filling together and set aside.

Divide the dough in half, roll one out to a circle 25 cm/10 inches in diameter. Using a crimped pastry wheel, cut the round into 14 wedges. Spread half the filling over the wedges, then roll up from the wide end. Place on a greased baking sheet. Repeat the procedure with the other half of dough and filling. Sprinkle with sugar and bake at 180°C/350°F/Gas Mark 4 for 20 minutes until golden.

EASTER CURRANT COOKIES

The rum glaze on these cookies makes them very special. Substitute orange juice if making them for children.

◆ ◆ ◆

175 G/6 OZ BUTTER OR MARGARINE

175 G/6 OZ CASTER SUGAR

1 EGG, BEATEN

30 ML/2 TBSP RUM

50 G/2 OZ MIXED PEEL, CHOPPED

100 G/4 OZ CURRANTS

350 G/12 OZ PLAIN FLOUR

5 ML/1 TSP MIXED SPICE

GLAZE

100 G/4 OZ ICING SUGAR

15 ML/1 TBSP DARK RUM

30 ML/2 TBSP APRICOT JAM, WARMED

MAKES ABOUT 24

◆ ◆ ◆

Put the butter or margarine into a bowl with the sugar and beat together until light and fluffy. Beat in the egg and rum. Stir in the mixed peel and currants, then sift in the flour and spices. Mix together to make a firm dough. Knead lightly until smooth.

Roll out the dough to 5 mm/$\frac{1}{4}$ inch thick and use a 5 cm/2 inch cutter to stamp out the cookies. Place them on greased baking sheets and bake at 180°C/350°F/Gas Mark 4 for 10-15 minutes.

Meanwhile, sift the icing sugar into a bowl, add the rum and mix to make a runny glacé icing.

Remove the cookies from the oven, and while still hot, brush with the apricot jam and then with the glaze. Transfer to a wire rack to cool.

FESTIVE ORANGE BISCUITS

This is both an attractive and delicious biscuit which is worth making for a festive celebration, or to give as a gift.

◆ ◆ ◆

100 G/4 OZ UNSALTED BUTTER, SOFTENED

50 G/2 OZ ICING SUGAR

GRATED RIND OF 1 LARGE ORANGE

30 ML/2 TBSP ORANGE JUICE

175 G/6 OZ PLAIN FLOUR

TO DECORATE

50 G/2 OZ PLAIN CHOCOLATE

50 G/2 OZ WHITE CHOCOLATE

MAKES 15

◆ ◆ ◆

Beat the butter and icing sugar together until light and creamy, then beat in the orange rind and juice. Sift in the flour and mix to make a soft dough. Spoon the mixture into a piping bag fitted with a large star nozzle and pipe circles about 4.5 cm/3 inches in diameter onto greased baking sheets. Chill for about 45 minutes.

Bake the biscuits at 160°C/325°F/Gas Mark 3 for 10-12 minutes. Transfer to a wire rack to cool completely.

Melt the chocolates separately in bowls placed over simmering water. Place each in a small greaseproof paper piping bag and pipe drizzles over each biscuit. Leave to set.

TOP: *Festive Orange Biscuits*
BOTTOM: *Easter Currant Cookies*

HIGHLAND SHORTBREAD

This recipe can be made into different shapes of shortbread. If a mould is available, use to make a traditional shortbread for a Scottish-style biscuit. Alternatively, cut into small rounds and decorate.

◆ ◆ ◆

225 G/8 OZ BUTTER

100 G/4 OZ CASTER SUGAR

225 G/8 OZ PLAIN FLOUR

100 G/4 OZ GROUND RICE OR CORNFLOUR

2.5 ML/$\frac{1}{2}$ TSP GRATED NUTMEG

CASTER SUGAR TO DUST

MAKES 2 LARGE SHORTBREAD AND 16-20 SMALL ONES

◆ ◆ ◆

Put the butter and sugar into a bowl and beat until light and creamy. Sift in the flour, ground rice or cornflour and nutmeg and work by hand to make a soft dough. Knead the dough on a lightly floured surface.

Take one-third of the dough and roll out to a round approximately 18 cm/7 inch in diameter. Prick with a fork and pinch the edges. Place on a greased baking sheet. Mark into 8 pieces. Refrigerate for 1 hour.

Roll out the remaining dough about 3mm/$\frac{1}{8}$th inch thick and cut into rounds using a 7.5 cm/3 inch cutter. Place on greased baking sheets and prick the surfaces with a fork. Bake in the oven at 180°C/350°F/Gas Mark 4 for about 15 minutes – the large round will take 20-25 minutes – until pale golden. Sprinkle with caster sugar. Cool on the baking sheets for 15 minutes, then transfer to a wire rack to cool completely.

CHRISTMAS FRUIT AND NUT COOKIES

Let the children help make these cookies during their Christmas vacation, they will make a welcome change to mince pies!

◆ ◆ ◆

100 G/4 OZ SOFT MARGARINE

100 G/4 OZ LIGHT MUSCOVADO SUGAR, SIFTED

1 EGG, BEATEN

225 G/8 OZ SELF-RAISING FLOUR

5 ML/1 TSP MIXED SPICE

75 G/3 OZ READY-TO-EAT APRICOTS, CHOPPED

75 G/3 OZ GLACE CHERRIES, CHOPPED

75 G/3 OZ BLANCHED ALMONDS, SLIVERED

BEATEN EGG TO GLAZE

GRANULATED SUGAR TO DUST

MAKES 22-24

◆ ◆ ◆

Put the margarine and sugar into a bowl and beat together until creamy. Add the egg and beat again. Sift in the flour and spice, then add the apricots, cherries and 50 g/2 oz of the almonds. Mix all the ingredients together.

Drop desertspoonfuls of the mixture onto greased baking sheets and flatten the surface with a fork. Brush the tops of the cookies with beaten egg to glaze, then scatter over the remaining almonds.

Bake at 180°C/350°F/Gas Mark 4 for 15-20 minutes until golden. Transfer to a wire rack to cool. If wished, the tops can be sprinkled with a little granulated sugar.

TOP: *Highland Shortbread*

BOTTOM: *Christmas Fruit and Nut Cookies*

LEBKUCHEN

*Spicy German Lebkuchen are traditionally
eaten on St Nicholas Day, December 6th.*

◆ ◆ ◆

3 EGGS
200 G/7 OZ CASTER SUGAR
175 G/6 OZ GROUND ALMONDS
50 G/2 OZ CANDIED PEEL, FINELY CHOPPED
50 G/2 OZ PLAIN FLOUR
5 ML/1 TSP CINNAMON
2.5 ML/½ TSP GROUND CARDAMON
GOOD PINCH OF GINGER, ALLSPICE AND
GROUND CLOVES

TO DECORATE
100 G/4 OZ PLAIN CHOCOLATE, MELTED
100 G/4 OZ ICING SUGAR
SUGAR STRANDS OR SPRINKLES

MAKES ABOUT 60

◆ ◆ ◆

Put the eggs and sugar into a bowl, stand over a pan of
simmering water and whisk until thick and foamy.
Remove the bowl from the pan and continue to whisk
for 2 minutes (or longer for thicker biscuits).

Combine the remaining ingredients together then stir
into the egg mixture. Drop heaped teaspoonfuls onto
baking sheets lined with non-stick baking parchment,
spreading them gently into smooth mounds. Bake at
160°C/325°F/Gas Mark 3 for 15-20 minutes, until light
brown and slightly soft to the touch. Slide the biscuits
onto wire racks to cool. Peel off the paper when cold.

Mix the icing sugar with a little water to make a thin
glaze, dip half of the cookies in this and the rest in the
melted chocolate. Sprinkle with sugar decorations.

CANE COOKIES

*These are fun cookies for children – super
for parties. Tie ribbons around them and
hang them on the Christmas tree.*

◆ ◆ ◆

175 G/6 OZ SOFT MARGARINE
75 G/3 OZ ICING SUGAR
5 ML/1 TSP GRATED LEMON RIND
25 G/1 OZ CORNFLOUR
200 G/7 OZ PLAIN FLOUR
15 ML/1 TBSP MILK
TO DECORATE
175 G/6 OZ ICING SUGAR
SUGAR STRANDS OR 'HUNDREDS AND THOUSANDS'

MAKES ABOUT 20

◆ ◆ ◆

Put the margarine and sugar into a bowl and beat until
soft and creamy. Add the lemon rind. Sift in the cornflour and flour and mix to a soft dough, using the milk
if necessary.

Place the mixture in a piping bag fitted with a star
nozzle and pipe walking cane shapes about 10 cm/4
inches long onto greased baking trays. Chill.

Bake at 190°C/375°F/Gas Mark 5 for 10-12 minutes
until pale golden. Transfer to a wire rack to cool.

Mix the icing sugar with enough water to make a
runny glacé icing and either dip the cookies in or brush
the icing over the tops. Finish with a scattering of sugar
decorations on each and allow to set.

TOP: *Cane Cookies*
BOTTOM: *Lebkuchen*

CINNAMON STARS

Children will love to help make these cookies, which can be cut into different shapes and hung on the Christmas tree.

◆ ◆ ◆

225 G/8 OZ SELF-RAISING FLOUR

15 ML/1 TBSP GROUND CINNAMON

175 G/6 OZ BUTTER

100 G/4 OZ CASTER SUGAR

5 ML/1 TSP GRATED ORANGE RIND

1 SMALL EGG, BEATEN

TO DECORATE

225 G/8 OZ ICING SUGAR

25-30 ML/5-6 TSP ORANGE JUICE

SUGAR STRANDS OR SILVER BALLS

MAKES ABOUT 36-40

◆ ◆ ◆

Sift the flour and cinnamon into a bowl, rub in the butter until the mixture resembles fine crumbs. Stir in the sugar and orange rind, then bind together with the egg.

Knead the dough on a lightly floured surface then cut out shapes such as stars, moons and Christmas trees, placing them on greased baking sheets. If wished, make a hole in each cookie with a skewer to thread with ribbon after baking and hang on the tree.

Bake the biscuits at 180°C/350°F/Gas Mark 4 for 12-15 minutes. Transfer to a wire rack to cool.

Blend the orange juice into the icing sugar to make a thick icing, then use to spread over the biscuits. Decorate with sugar strands or silver balls.

FESTIVE SPICY TWISTS

Make plenty of these cookies and put some in a pretty box to give away.

◆ ◆ ◆

300 G/10 OZ SELF-RAISING FLOUR

7.5 ML/1$\frac{1}{2}$ TSP MIXED SPICE

2.5 ML/$\frac{1}{2}$ TSP GROUND GINGER

150 G/5 OZ BUTTER

100 G/4 0Z LIGHT MUSCOVADO SUGAR,

SIFTED

1 EGG, BEATEN

ICING SUGAR TO DUST

MAKES 20

◆ ◆ ◆

Sift the flour and spices into a bowl. Add the butter and rub in until the mixture resembles fine crumbs. Stir in the sugar then bind to a dough with the egg.

Divide the mixture into 20 pieces. Take each piece and roll into a rope about 20 cm/8 inches long, then fold in half and twist.

Place the twists on greased baking sheets and refrigerate for 30 minutes.

Bake the cookies at 180°C/350°F/Gas Mark 4 for 12-15 minutes or until golden. Transfer to a wire rack to cool, then dust with icing sugar.

TOP: *Cinnamon Stars*
BOTTOM: *Festive Spicy Twists*

NO-BAKE COOKIES

These are not cookies in the true sense, but they are so irresistible and so easy to make that it is well worth having a selection of recipes to choose from. Children will love making these as they use many of the most popular ingredients, including chocolate. Cooking is great fun for children, but basic safety in the kitchen is very important. Remind children to wash their hands before starting to prepare food and make sure you supervise young children while they are melting chocolate or using sharp knives to chop food or cut up cookies.

Follow the recipes carefully and always weigh the ingredients; don't guess the measurements. When measuring syrup, it is helpful to rinse a tablespoon in very hot water before use, so that the syrup slides easily off the spoon. In some recipes the chocolate is melted in a saucepan with other ingredients. Otherwise, to melt chocolate, place in a bowl over a pan of simmering water, taking care not to let the water boil or splash into the bowl or the chocolate will become thick and grainy.

Once prepared, these cookies are refrigerated until firm and are best stored in the refrigerator until needed to prevent them softening. Most of the recipes are ideal to make for children's parties, with one or two more sophisticated ones, such as Belgian Chocolate Slices, which could be served after dinner with coffee.

CONTENTS

♦ ♦ ♦

Chocolate Biscuit Treats
Golden Crackles
Coconut Dreams   88

Bubble Bars
Apricot Clusters
Butterscotch Fingers   90

Cherry Nut Bites
Belgian Chocolate Slices
Nutty Fudge Triangles   92

CHOCOLATE BISCUIT TREATS

◆ ◆ ◆

225 G/8 OZ MILK CHOCOLATE

100 G/4 OZ BUTTER

30 ML/2 TBSP GOLDEN SYRUP

175 G/6 OZ DIGESTIVE BISCUITS, ROUGHLY BROKEN

50 G/2 OZ RAISINS OR SULTANAS

50 G/2 OZ FLAKED ALMONDS, LIGHTLY TOASTED

25 G/1 OZ GLACE CHERRIES, FINELY CHOPPED

MAKES 12

◆ ◆ ◆

Put the chocolate, butter and syrup into a pan and heat very gently until melted. Stir in the biscuits, raisins and almonds. Turn into a greased 18 cm/7 inch shallow square tin and level the surface. Scatter over the chopped cherries and refrigerate to set. Cut into bars or squares.

GOLDEN CRACKLES

◆ ◆ ◆

50 G /2 OZ BUTTER

30 ML/2 TBSP GOLDEN SYRUP

100 G/4 OZ MILK CHOCOLATE

50 G/2 OZ CORNFLAKES

25 G/1 OZ PEANUT KERNELS, CHOPPED

MAKES 12

◆ ◆ ◆

Put the butter, syrup and chocolate into a pan. Heat gently until melted then remove from the heat and stir in the cornflakes and nuts. Divide the mixture between 12 paper cases and refrigerate until set.

COCONUT DREAMS

◆ ◆ ◆

100 G/4 OZ BUTTER

225 G/8 OZ SHORTCAKE BISCUITS, CRUSHED

25 G/1 OZ COCOA

150 G/5 OZ CASTER SUGAR

90 ML/3 FL OZ SINGLE CREAM

175 G/6 OZ DESICCATED COCONUT

3 TBSP CRUSHED PINEAPPLE, WELL DRAINED

175 G/6 OZ PLAIN CHOCOLATE

40 G/1$^{1}/_{2}$ OZ BUTTER

MAKES 18

◆ ◆ ◆

Melt the butter, then mix in the crushed biscuits and cocoa. Press into the base of a 23 cm/9 inch shallow square tin, lined with non-stick baking parchment. Refrigerate until firm.

Put the sugar and cream into a saucepan, stir over a low heat for 3-4 minutes. Cool slightly then stir in the coconut and pineapple and spread over the base.

For the topping, put the chocolate and butter into a bowl over a pan of simmering water and stir until melted. Spread over the filling then set in the refrigerator.

Use a hot knife to cut into squares.

TOP: *Chocolate Biscuit Treats*
BOTTOM LEFT: *Coconut Dreams*
BOTTOM RIGHT: *Golden Crackles*

BUBBLE BARS

◆ ◆ ◆

75 G/3 OZ BUTTER

175 G/6 OZ MARSHMALLOWS

75 G/3 OZ MILK CHOCOLATE

100 G/4 OZ RICE CRISPIES

MAKES 18

◆ ◆ ◆

Put the butter, marshmallows and chocolate into a pan, place over a low heat and allow to melt. Remove from the heat and stir in the rice crispies. Turn into a greased 18 x 28 cm/7 x 11 inch shallow baking tin and press evenly. Leave to set then cut into bars.

APRICOT CLUSTERS

◆ ◆ ◆

100 G/4 OZ BUTTER

30 ML/2 TBSP GOLDEN SYRUP

100 G/4 OZ MILK CHOCOLATE

100 G/4 OZ READY-TO-EAT DRIED APRICOTS, CHOPPED

175 G/6 OZ CRUNCHY OAT CEREAL, LIGHTLY CRUSHED

MAKES 12

◆ ◆ ◆

Melt the butter with the golden syrup and chocolate, allow to cool. Stir in the apricots and cereal then divide between 12 paper cases. Refrigerate to set.

BUTTERSCOTCH FINGERS

◆ ◆ ◆

75 G/3 OZ BUTTER

75 G/3 OZ LIGHT MUSCOVADO SUGAR, SIFTED

15 ML/1 TBSP GOLDEN SYRUP

75 G/3 OZ RAISINS

50 G/2 OZ HAZELNUTS, CHOPPED

100 G/4 OZ DIGESTIVE BISCUITS, LIGHTLY CRUSHED

5O G/2 OZ GLACE CHERRIES, CHOPPED

25 G/1 OZ MIXED PEEL

MAKES 14

◆ ◆ ◆

Put the butter, sugar and syrup into a pan. Heat gently until the sugar dissolves, stirring all the time. Increase the heat and simmer for 2 minutes.

Stir in the remaining ingredients and mix well. Turn into a greased 18 cm/7 inch shallow square tin and refrigerate to set. Cut into fingers to serve.

TOP: *Apricot Clusters*
BOTTOM LEFT: *Bubble Bars*
BOTTOM RIGHT: *Butterscotch Fingers*

CHERRY NUT BITES

❖ ❖ ❖

175 G/6 OZ WHITE CHOCOLATE
50 G/2 OZ MIXED NUTS, CHOPPED AND
LIGHTLY TOASTED
100 G/4 OZ DESICCATED COCONUT
100 G/4 OZ GLACE CHERRIES, CHOPPED

M A K E S   1 6

❖ ❖ ❖

Place the chocolate in a bowl over a pan of simmering water and stir until melted. Stir in the remaining ingredients then turn into a 18 cm/7 inch shallow square tin, lined with non-stick baking parchment. Refrigerate until set then cut into squares.

BELGIAN CHOCOLATE SLICES

❖ ❖ ❖

225 G/8 OZ PLAIN CHOCOLATE
75 G/3 OZ UNSALTED BUTTER
15 ML/1 TBSP GOLDEN SYRUP
30 ML/2 TBSP SINGLE CREAM
75 G/3 OZ GLACE PINEAPPLE
75 G/3 OZ WALNUTS OR PECANS, CHOPPED
100 G/4 OZ COCONUT BISCUITS, LIGHTLY CRUSHED
2 TBSP DESICCATED OR SHREDDED COCONUT

M A K E S   1 6   S L I C E S

❖ ❖ ❖

Put the chocolate, butter and syrup into a pan and heat gently until melted. Remove from the heat and stir the cream, glacé pineapple, nuts and biscuit in. Press evenly into a 20 cm/8 inch greased loose-bottomed flan tin. Refrigerate to set. Remove the tin, decorate the edge with the coconut then cut into slices.

NUTTY FUDGE TRIANGLES

❖ ❖ ❖

50 G/2 OZ BUTTER
100 G/4 OZ MILK CHOCOLATE
225 G/8 OZ DIGESTIVE BISCUITS, CRUSHED
T O P P I N G
75 G/3 OZ BUTTER
397 G/14 OZ CAN CONDENSED MILK
100 G/4 OZ FUDGE FINGER BARS
50 G/2 0Z NUTS, CHOPPED AND LIGHTLY TOASTED

M A K E S   3 0

❖ ❖ ❖

Put the butter and chocolate into a pan, stir over a low heat until melted. Mix in the crushed biscuits then press evenly into a greased 18 x 28 cm/7 x 11 inch shallow tin. Refrigerate until set.

For the topping, put the butter and condensed milk into a saucepan, bring to simmer, stirring, and cook for 4-5 minutes until very thick. Break up the fudge bars, add to the pan and stir until melted. Pour over the base then scatter over the nuts. Refrigerate until set. Cut into 15 squares then cut each in half to make triangles.

TOP: *Cherry Nut Bites*
CENTRE: *Nutty Fudge Triangles*
BOTTOM: *Belgian Chocolate Slices*

INDEX

Almond bakewells, cherry 66
Almond crisps 18
Anzacs 18
Apple cinnamon crumbles 70
Apricot:
    Apricot almandines 50
    Apricot clusters 90
    Apricot cookies, poppyseed 58
    Apricot sables 26

Banana pecan cookies 10
Belgian chocolate slices 92
Bubble bars 90
Butter biscuits, Italian 22
Butter cookies:
    Date butter cookies 56
    Jam-filled butter cookies 32
Butterscotch:
    Butterscotch biscuits 42
    Butterscotch fingers 90

Cane cookies 82
Cherry:
    Cherry almond bakewells 66
    Cherry garlands 36
    Cherry nut bites 92
Chocolate:
    Belgian chocolate slices 92
    Bubble bars 90
    Chocolate biscuit treats 88
    Chocolate caramels 62
    Chocolate chunk and nut
      cookies 30
    Chocolate marzipan whirls 46

Chocolate orange pinwheels 16
Chocolate pecan bars 58
Chocolate pistachio fancies 44
Double chocolate chip cookies 10
Striped chocolate and vanilla
    cookies 14
Christmas fruit and nut cookies 80
Cinnamon:
    Apple cinnamon crumbles 70
    Cinnamon stars 84
    Dutch cinnamon biscuits 64
Coconut:
    Anzacs 18
    Coconut crunchies 14
    Coconut dreams 88
    Coconut macaroons 22
    Coconut squares 68
    Coconut tuiles 44
Coffee:
    Coffee cream crumbles 50
    Coffee date swirls 40
Cream cheese cookies 76
Crystallized ginger creams 46
Currant cookies, Easter 78

Date:
    Coffee date swirls 40
    Date butter cookies 56
Double chocolate chip cookies 10
Dutch cinnamon biscuits 64
Dutch shortcakes 28

Easter currant cookies 78

Festive orange biscuits 78
Festive spicy twists 84
Figgy rolls 60
Flapjacks, hazelnut 62

Florentines 40
Fruit and nut cookies, Christmas 80
Fudge triangles, nutty 92

Ginger:
    Crystallized ginger creams 46
    Festive spicy twists 84
    Ginger snaps 16
Gingerbread folk 20
Glazed lemon shorties 70
Golden crackles 88

Hazelnut dollars 28
Hazelnut flapjacks 62
Highland shortbread 80
Honey jumbles 26

Irish lace cookies 48
Italian butter biscuits 22

Jam-filled butter cookies 32

Lebkuchen 82
Lemon:
    Glazed lemon shorties 70
    Lemon refrigerator biscuits 12
    Lemon shells 12
Linzer bars, strawberry 56

Macaroons, coconut 22
Madeleine cookies, orange 36
Maple hearts, pecan and 52
Marmalade crunchies 60
Marzipan:
    Chocolate marzipan whirls 46
    Coconut Macaroons 22
    Marzipan lattice cookies 38
Melting moments 30

Meringue hearts and kisses 74
Mocha slices 52

Nuts:
 Almond crisps 18
 Apple cinnamon crumbles 70
 Apricot almandines 50
 Apricot sables 26
 Banana pecan cookies 10
 Butterscotch fingers 90
 Cherry almond bakewells 66
 Cherry nut bites 92
 Chocolate biscuit treats 88
 Chocolate chunk and nut
  cookies 30
 Chocolate pecan bars 58
 Chocolate pistachio fancies 44
 Christmas fruit and nut cookies 80
 Coffee date swirls 40
 Cream cheese cookies 76
 Double chocolate chip cookies 10
 Florentines 40
 Hazelnut dollars 28
 Hazelnut flapjacks 62
 Honey jumbles 26
 Lebkuchen 82
 Marmalade crunchies 60
 Nutty crescents 48

Nutty fudge triangles 92
Nutty honey diamonds 66
Peanut crunchies 32
Pecan and maple hearts 52
Poppyseed pouches 76
Strawberry linzer bars 56
Valentine knots 74
Walnut curls 42

Oatmeal raisin cookies 24
Oaty shortbread 24
Orange:
 Chocolate orange pinwheels 16
 Festive orange biscuits 78
 Orange madeleine cookies 36

Peanut crunchies 32
Pecan:
 Banana pecan cookies 10
 Chocolate pecan bars 58
 Pecan and maple hearts 52
Pistachio fancies, chocolate 44
Poppyseed apricot cookies 58
Poppyseed pouches 76

Raisin cookies, oatmeal 24
Refrigerator biscuits, lemon 12

Sesame triangles 68
Shortbread:
 Apricot sables 26
 Dutch shortcakes 28
 Glazed lemon shorties 70
 Highland shortbread 80
 Oaty shortbread 24
Spicy twists, festive 84
Strawberry linzer bars 56

Tutti frutti squares 64

Valentine knots 74
Vanilla:
 Striped chocolate and vanilla
  cookies 14
 Vanilla sugar cookies 20
Viennese fingers 38

Walnut curls 42

ACKNOWLEDGMENTS

The author and publishers
would like to thank the following for their help
in the preparation of this book:

BERNDES
for supplying small cookie cutters

BILLINGTONS
for supplying unrefined sugars

LAKELAND PLASTICS
for supplying Airbake Cookie sheets